THE

GLOBAL

BLACK MAN

GETTING OUT OF THE HOOD AND GOOD IN THE WORLD

by

Alexis Neal

A reconciliation of multiple perspectives and experiences of the world through the lens of a disadvantaged but determined young man from the South Side of Chicago, a Black retired US Army officer, a high school teacher, and a businessman in Kansas City, Missouri.

Biography of Alexis Neal

Lex is a resident of Kansas City, Missouri, and a businessperson in the marijuana industry. He is father to three beautiful humans—Kacie, Nele, and Thelonious—and grandfather to Baby Bella. Lex is a retired US Army officer. He was promoted to the rank of colonel shortly before his retirement, having served a total of 28 years, 5 months, and 25 days of military service. Lex has worn the uniform of the American Soldier since he was 12, as a freshman at Chicago Vocational High School, when he enrolled in JROTC. After retiring from the Army, Lex returned to instruct JROTC at Central High School in KCMO.

My journey began at a young age when I was faced with challenging circumstances in my own neighborhood. Growing up in Woodlawn, I witnessed violence, poverty, drug and alcohol abuse on a daily basis. This environment had a profound impact on my mental well-being and self-esteem. To escape the negativity surrounding me, I turned to education. Despite my stutter, I immersed myself in learning and focused on improving my communication skills. This dedication paid off after I was accepted into the Army's National Guard program. However, the transition from my troubled neighborhood to the disciplined military environment presented its own set of challenges. Additionally, I grappled with the psychological toll of being a minority in a predominantly white institution.

I used these challenges as fuel for self-improvement and sought out mentors, both inside and outside the military, who could guide me and provide the positive influence I longed for during my life. These mentors helped me navigate the military system and instilled the values of resilience, determination, and dedication. During my military career, I faced numerous obstacles and setbacks, but most times I persevered. I made it a personal mission to challenge the stereotypes associated with young African American men. This biography communicates my unique perspective from what I consider... a unique individual.

Foreword

I have held many titles throughout my life: warrior, soldier, entrepreneur, artist, teacher, failed husband a few times, mentor, and self-proclaimed student of the world. Out of all of these, the one that means the absolute most is father! I am a father to my beautiful Kacie Rian Alverson, Nele Alyssa Neal, and Thelonius Alexander Neal, and grandfather to Baby Bella. I've taken the time to capture my thoughts about my life and how my history may help communicate some important aspects of the life challenges of being a Black man in America to my son.

I believe that I will be there to help guide and raise my son to be a Global Black Man. That is my aspiration, but sometimes things don't turn out the way we would like them to. This isn't for everybody. It is specific for young Black men. Specific for young Black men in urban environments. Specific for those who often see the future with a pervasive lack of hope—those who don't have the hope to live the American Dream.

But this is not the dream of the cute house in the suburbs with a white picket fence, 2.5 kids, and a two-car garage. The real American Dream is described in the Preamble to our Constitution, which starts with "We the People." Unfortunately, "we" were not included in the proverbial "we," and although I spent over 32 years in uniform as a member of the US military, from high school JROTC to teaching high school JROTC, I haven't always felt that I've been included as part of "the people" with the full rights and privileges as an American citizen. Sadly, I feel that I wasn't accepted as an American until after 9/11.

My perception of life as a Black man in America is shaped by my unique set of interpersonal skills, which close distances and foster intimacy; a successful career that cultivated expeditionary travel; and a traumatic history both in my personal life and in combat and training environments. This perception is now shaped by a very optimistic outlook on life. There were good days and there were bad days, but there will always be a better day.

Until 9/11, 9 out of 10 times I flew commercially, I was randomly searched and randomly selected for additional screening. I was randomly pulled over while driving and randomly surveyed in nearly every high-end store. Because of my unique personality and soft smile, which often hid my own insecurities, people frequently accepted the chipmunk cheeks for what they were and befriended me. These characteristics provided me with unique opportunities to travel and experience the world in a way that was different from most.

My son, and all sons who have been and will be Black men in America, the world is growing, often without us. We must be part of the world to help foster the real narrative of our beauty, creativity, vitality, and critical thinking abilities as African Americans. There is more to us than hip-hop, sports, and fashion. The only way the narrative changes is when we change it, when we break stereotypes and create real, meaningful relationships.

My observations lead me to believe that some of us have taken on the perspective to not care about things outside our direct control. Even after Reconstruction, Jim Crow, the Civil Rights Movement, and the first Black president, some African Americans still won't get involved in politics, don't care about world events, never had a conversation with people from other religions about religion, or hold healthy discussions about investments and finances. Why?

- "It don't matter."
- "Nothing's gonna change anyway."
- "They don't give a fuck about me, so why should I give a fuck about them?"

Why? Because the world has developed and will continue to develop without our input. Many times, my engagements with other cultures with limited or no experience with African American culture are filled with exaggerations, false narratives, and just flat-out wrong legends, which "they" heard from "reliable" sources.

When I was younger and my brothers were reaching their teen years, I wrote "21 Rules to Live by" for them and posted it in my mother's kitchen. It was generally some things I felt would provide them with some foundations to assist them into manhood. I wish the men in my life had been more deliberate about Black men raising Black men. As I grew older, the 21 became 42, not because I gained double the insight, but because I began to look for positive role models to help guide me through what would be a successful, rewarding, and at times traumatic career. "42" at the time was based upon the history and life of Jackie Robinson, number 42. I don't think I actually wrote 42 rules down; most were just repetitiously worded to equal 42 rules to live by. The repetition emphasizes influence on particular areas. Then I realized there are many more than 42, hundreds maybe, because at points throughout my 28-year career, I wrote some things down. I have at least 5 dozen notebooks, journals, and sketchbooks in boxes and drawers; once I see them, I'm captured for hours revisiting where I was when I was there.

Throughout my military career, I often found myself as the only Black officer in groups with my peers and seniors. Some of the time, these men whom I admired and respected didn't really understand me, take the time to understand where I was coming from, or care to know the external stress I carried. I can only remember a couple of engagements where I talked to my commander about myself and my history. Most of my commanders weren't interested in "me" personally and what motivated me; they were interested in my contributions to the success of the organization. I got used to seniors not investigating, then peers. Eventually, most people only knew the basics about me because I kept my story to myself and also hid my depression and other pains I was experiencing. There have been a handful of people who have touched me in a deep and meaningful way, and I'm fortunate for those few.

In my very early lieutenant years, some superiors made racial jokes. Although it made me feel uncomfortable, I accepted it because that was just the way things were. By the end of the 1990s, most of the racial comments and gestures would be limited to other-than-Black ethnic jokes or stereotypes. With a heavy heart and guilt, I was happy that it wasn't me. Although they weren't joking about Blacks in my presence, I knew they probably did when I wasn't around. You wouldn't believe how many times I heard, "Hey Lex, I need to tell you this joke, but you gotta promise me that you won't get offended. It's about race, but it's really funny though, want to hear it?"

With some seniors or peers, inevitably, they feel right NOW is the time and place to have the infamous "N word" conversation. That time and place were usually under the influence of alcohol. You know the conversation that starts off with, "Sooooo, why can comedians and rappers say the N word but I can't?" My response: "You can say whatever you want to say to whomever you want to say it to. You just have to be ready for whatever consequence or reaction that transpires after that. Besides, why do you want to say nigger?" Usually, there's a bunch of backtracking and "I was just wondering" and "That's not what I said."

Now take that external stress and multiply it by my misguided self-declaration that I, Alexis Neal, would single-handedly change the perspective of African American culture for the entire military. The reality is that I suffered from an inferiority complex when I compared myself with my caucasian counterparts. It would take an entire career for me to fully understand why I believed I needed to work harder and present a strong facade without perceivable signs of weakness.

I was inferior, but not physically or mentally, but in an inequitable way. I began much further behind the starting line than most of my peers when the gun shot off. A very small population of my peers, regardless of race, shared similar background stories of their tumultuous upbringings, and they too started behind the line.

There were a lot of things I had to catch up on to gain worldly experience to become equals with my peers, but intelligence, hard work, and determination would not be an excuse for not being at least equitably measured with my peers.

I am who I am because of how I ran the race and how that race reciprocated effects back onto me. I hope I get to review this essay with my son as he prepares to make his mark on the world. My Nele can attest that this is how I live my life. It wasn't and will never be perfect. There were good days that I reminisce about, mostly about experiences with family and friends. There were some bad days that I try not to recall, because they make me depressed remembering close friends who didn't finish the race. But one day my son will read this essay, and he will approach this world believing that there will always be a better day.

The purpose of this essay is not to exclude anyone but to include a specific demographic into the rest of the world. I believe it is essential to consider where you want to be in life and then create a plan to get you there. If I want to drive across the country, I make a plan. I do some research to find out where I want to stay, things and people I want to see, and experiences I want to have along the way. My suggestion is simple: Make a plan for your life that gets you from where you are and has those critical milestones to get you to where you want to be.

Table of Contents

Artifacts of our Past

The world is evolving, our societies are evolving, and our values and beliefs are evolving—not getting worse. Artifacts of our past are those physical, emotional, and psychological tools and baggage we carry that define us as people. These artifacts help us to understand our history and learn from it, but we should not limit ourselves to reliving our history of glory days. Humanity is evolving to a more enlightened and just society. The Bible is full of verses instructing slaves to submit and obey their masters, whether they are good or evil. When I was a young lieutenant, my company commander made racial jokes. We had scantily clad posters of women in offices, restrooms, and mechanic bays. Until recently, the majority of the U.S. population would have never accepted same-sex marriage. I believe the world will be a much more tolerant and just place in the future, void of radicals and racism, similar to the place Dr. Martin Luther King Jr. preached about. Today, we easily acknowledge that the Holocaust, slavery, and even the Crusades were horrible moments in history, just as future generations will look to the great scandals of the presidential elections of 2020 for reference and inspiration.

Some of us, such as I, held on to one such artifact: the N word. For most of my adult life, I've had a visceral response when I heard the word in public. I hated hearing it when I was walking through the airport in Nuremberg, Germany, and a 3-year-old kid started pointing at me and saying "a nigger" over and over while the mother tried to cover the child's mouth. I didn't like being pulled over and asked by a white officer, "Why is a nigger like you driving through my town?" I used to cringe when I was at a public music event and heard Jamie Foxx open up with, "She takes my money when I'm in need," waiting for what seemed like forever to find out which version the DJ was playing.

I suppose that many things I cared about when I was young, I no longer have the same intolerance for. And, contrarily, some things I just can't tolerate at all, period, not even a little bit. In order to take a journey, you have to decide to take artifacts with you that will help you through your journey and leave the other things that burden your travel. As you progress through this journey, be prepared to exchange more efficient and effective artifacts or code-switch. When you do make those changes, know the value of *you* as part of the exchange.

My Inspiration

The atmosphere during the spring and summer of 2008 was electric. This was shortly after I started to reconnect with my mother, and we shared long conversations about the very impressive presidential candidate from my hometown of Chicago. My mother was excited. She often expressed that she didn't think she would live long enough to see a Black American president. Mom was "Moms" again instead of my mother, and it felt good. Unfortunately, Moms never did get to see Barack Obama win the election or witness his inauguration. Eddie Mae Bynum died in August 2008 from heart complications. I was notified by my instructor while I was in class at the School for Advanced Military Studies. I cried for eight hours from Leavenworth, Kansas, to Turrell, Arkansas, because I missed the opportunity to fully reconcile with my mom. This is why I'm not afraid to tell my family and friends, I love you!

My mother endured poverty, she persevered through Jim Crow South, experiencing violent and institutional racism her entire life, she survived being abandoned, physical, emotional and psychological abuse, even being shot by my father, and having her home and artistic center burned down by my brothers' father, but she did not survive NOT having health insurance or live long enough to see President Obama take office.

Barack Obama, Malcolm X, Martin Luther King, Jackie Robinson, and Ellis "Sun" Bynum are the men who inspired me the most. Curtis Taylor and Thomas Guthrie are the two leaders who truly invested in me and challenged me to excel. My purpose—Thelonius Alexander Neal and Baby Bella—and my inspiration—Nele Alyssa Neal and Kacie Rian Alverson: My world revolves around you.

The Early Influence

Despite seemingly insurmountable skepticism and open doubting, even from my closest family members, I made it not only out of the hood but into the global community. As a commissioned officer in the US Army, I traveled A LOT. I met some wonderful people who became friends/family, admired the wonders of the world, and partied like a rockstar. I've loved beautiful women; fought, won, and lost battles both figuratively and literally; challenged my moral fiber; and been both inspired by the creator and lost faith in such. The path I traveled wasn't easy; there wasn't a map from the South Side of Chicago that led me to Kansas City. It was a hard and persistent hustle.

I come from a long line of hustlers, and there have been several who have had an impact on me. My grandfather, Sun Bynum, was the grandson of a slave who taught his sons to hustle by any means necessary, legit or not. Sun Bynum was a giant of a man who instilled in me a strong ethic for work. My uncles were real men who had a mystical presence. Uncle Sonny lived close to or with my grandparents down in Turrell, Arkansas, for as long as I can remember. He was the one who taught me to hunt and fight. I remember asking him to teach me to fight when I was about 7. He told me, "Put yo hands up," then solidly punched me in the face, causing my nose to gush blood and my eyes to swell. His response: "First rule about fighting, little nigga, keep yo hands up." Lesson 1, check! Uncle Ellis lived in Chicago near us with part of his family. He owned a concrete construction company and was this supercool cat who always had a fat stack in his pocket and a much younger woman on his arm. Once, he and I went on a double date with these two sisters. I had just turned 16 and went with the 17-year-old, and Ellis took the 19-year-old. Uncle Ray—think Shaft! He was so freaking cool that I swear he had theme music when he walked.

Before he was murdered, he was my favorite uncle. Uncle RC currently lives in California and was always on the periphery of our family, but always had positive conversations about the world. He is the last living uncle and the patriarch of our family.

William James Neal was my father, but the legacy doesn't start here. Neal, as I called him, lived most time less than a quarter-mile away from me and was the man who had the most significant impact on my life. He was a raging alcoholic, shot my mother, physically and mentally abused every woman he was ever in a relationship with, paid zero in child support, gave zero in emotional support, and even though he fathered over 20 children, didn't participate in raising them. I visited my father several months before he died, after one of my sisters let me know he wasn't doing well. I drove 12 hours to Mississippi and visited with him for a few hours. I thought I would feel something, but I didn't. I don't miss him. I stopped missing him a very long time ago.

When I was about 14, Moms brought Cleveland Jones Jr. home after her visit to Turrell for the funeral of a childhood friend. Cousin Cleve, as he was described, quickly went from a relative staying a few days to being Moms' boyfriend and soon-to-be husband. Stepfather Cleve's presence initiated my sister Sonya moving out and, subsequently, Moms moving from Chicago to Arkansas. Initially, Moms told me they were going to Arkansas for the weekend. The weekend became a week, then two. Then one day, Moms showed up, packed some things, gave me $100, and said they were moving to Arkansas.

This was not the right time for a Black 16-year-old boy to live by himself in Chicago. Shortly before that, my three best friends all went away to prison after pleading guilty to charges of murder. Now, in my junior year of high school, I was working full time at my "part-time" job at a fast-food restaurant. This popular restaurant didn't pay enough, but true to the hustle, I found a way—at the expense of the restaurant and a crooked manager who developed a slick scheme to undercharge customers and split the excess at the end of the night. That was until we got caught and several of us lost our employment. Fortunately, he was the only one who faced charges. By the end of 11th grade, I was doing so horribly in school and life that I was at risk of repeating the grade. Instead, I convinced my mother to let me move to Arkansas to make up for the nearly failing grades. I spent the last year at Turrell High School, which I could see from the back porch of my grandfather's house.

After I'd lived at Cleveland's house for about two weeks, Moms kicked me out because Cleveland and I got into a physical altercation. So, I spent my last year as a child at my grandfather's house. There, I would spend time with the man who influenced my life the most and instilled a strong sense of work ethic and family.

Several things will always haunt me, and despite counseling, I've never been able to let them go. One of those is how my grandfather turned his back on me when I decided to go to college. He attempted to align our family against me and told them that I stole his pocket watch. Years after my grandfather died, my Aunt Dean gave me the watch and told me all the negative things my grandfather said. She told me that she didn't believe it at the time, and she felt I deserved to have that watch. The funniest thing about the whole situation: I never remembered seeing the pocket watch before my aunt gave it to me. I still have it. It's not worth much and it doesn't work, but I hold on to this artifact of my past.

The second artifact I hold on to is a memory of my soon-to-be stepfather giving me a haircut. In our first real conversation, he asked me what I was going to be when I grew up. I responded that I wanted to go to college and become an architect. I distinctly remember the doubt he expressed and the words he spoke. He said, "College, huh, OK. Like the blind man said, we'll see…" Almost two decades later, Cleveland and I revisited that conversation, and that was the first time I heard sincerity from him with regard to me. He apologized for doubting me and was proud of my accomplishments, which led to me being promoted to major and selected to attend the Command and General Staff College.

The last artifact still has a tremendous effect on me and has crafted my relationship with my wonderful and beautiful daughter, Nele. It's not a specific moment or event but a collection of events, engagements, phone calls, and requests. Growing up, I saw my father sometimes every day, but I can only remember one time when my father was my father. When I was 5 or 6, I had pneumonia, and he carried me on his shoulders to each visit to the hospital. I can remember thinking *Dad* instead of *Neal*. Other than that, he was present but did not have a father. I am extremely thankful to Doris, Nele's mom, for allowing me to be a part of her life and for keeping Nele connected to me even when I was deployed. And finally, I'm thankful to Rick and Gail Alverson for adopting Kacie and raising her to be such a phenomenal young woman.

Here is an amazing story. I conducted an Ancestry DNA test to research vacation destinations I wanted to visit with my son. I wanted something to connect us to our African heritage. The results weren't too surprising: 47% Nigerian, 10% Scottish and Scandinavian, and 43% West African. Then I sent a message to the person with whom I shared a parent/child relationship. I thought to myself, this must be one of my father's children, not understanding what "parent/child" means.

I wrote, "It looks like we share some DNA," and left my email address.

Her response:

"Hi I just sent you an email"

"I just looked at our connection. I guess you are my father?"

"I look like you"

It took me a few moments to read, reread, and read again. Once I saw her picture, I knew immediately Kacie was my daughter. What a beautiful surprise! My dear sweet Nele went from being an only child for 19 years of her life to being a middle child. Kacie and

I met up within a couple of days and have been in each other's lives since.

Besides my mom, the most important female figure growing up was my sister Sonya B. Sonya practically raised me. As kids, we were always together. Mom was a single parent, but she taught us how to maneuver around Chicago using the public bus system. Sonya and I were known to travel all over Chicago using the bus and train system. We were legitimately poor—food stamps, government cheese, powdered milk, all of it—and sometimes Moms needed more help, which is where Arthur came into play. Arthur was a married man, but carried on with my mom and helped out with the bills. Everybody knew about their relationship, but it just wasn't talked about. Arthur was always around until about the time Moms hooked up again with her high school boyfriend, Cleveland.

Eddie Mae Bynum-Jones was my mother. In the early days of my life, it was just the three of us: Momma, Sonya, and me. To Sonya, I was her little brother, the one to be bossed around. To this day, Sonya still tries to boss me and my brothers around. Moms taught us to be independent, look both ways when crossing the street, be respectful, say please and thank you, and when it becomes necessary, knuckle up and fight for what you believe in and your family. Until I was 16, there was no woman who could ever take the place of Moms—until I was replaced. The hurt and betrayal I felt then negatively affected the next few decades of relationships.

Making it out of the hood is only a step, like graduating from high school. These small tasks should not be the most important accomplishments of your life. Graduating from high school should be as normal as riding a bike. As a high school teacher, I found it hard to get students to focus on the big picture of education: learning how to think. I used the analogy from "Karate Kid." Ralph in the first movie or Jaden in the second, it really doesn't matter; the story is the same. Both characters found themselves struggling to comply with Sensei's assignments because they couldn't quite understand the path. "Wax on, wax off...Jacket on, jacket off." I explained to students how algebra is used daily to understand which is the best decision to make when comparing unequal things.

We must make the cognitive shift from getting out of the hood or graduating from high school as our main objective to becoming active members of the global society, where we have the greatest impact on our world and potentially our galaxy as we explore space. The objective for young Black men becomes to influence the world's propensity through direct involvement in geoeconomics, geopolitics, geosocial, geocommunications, geologistics, geo everything. This is the desired effect of normalizing a Global Black Man across world markets.

The world is changing, the world is evolving, and the world is getting better. I hear a lot of supposedly higher cognitive and spiritual leaders assess sociological advancements such as gay marriage, sexual identity, immigration, and diversity as the tools that will cause the collapse of our society. But acceptance—treating people with dignity and respect despite their sexual identity, color of their skin, language spoken, regional accent, origination, and other preferences—cannot be why other hegemonic cultures failed. It is not why Rome failed. It is not why the sun now sets on the British Empire. It is the failure of the elites, noblemen, and religious zealots to accept change in their society. It will be our generation's greatest failure if we don't understand that the acceptance of diversity and elevating those who have been systematically disadvantaged is the best way toward "We the People of the United States, in order to form a more perfect union, establish justice, ensure domestic tranquility, provide for the common defense, promote the general welfare, and secure the blessings of liberty to ourselves and our posterity...."!

My son, I wish for you to be so much better human than I've been. I've been a miserable human to a lot of people in pursuit of the perfect mission. Theo and Baby Bella are my mission now: to facilitate these beautiful beings to love freely, pursue their passions, communicate openly, engage to be enlightened, find internal sources of their power, project with conviction, glare with amazement, challenge diplomatically, fight like a champion, win gracefully, accept defeat, punish wickedness, judge empathetically, and live their lives to the fullest.

I'm writing this essay just in case I am not there to watch you pursue your dreams and advise you along the way. My son, use these words to understand me, and the lessons I believe will help you through this life. Get yourself a good dog, because anything worth having is worth the investment and the sacrifice. Training a dog is the best lesson in humility and being a human. A dog, true and loyal, will let you know when he's being mistreated. He will demand more and more but knows when he's had enough—but will always ask, just in case. With a simple nudge, a dog will let you know when you are outside of your boundaries. Get yourself a dog, son; he'll always listen sympathetically and be there for you when everyone else won't. The greatest gift that I can give you is the gift of dreaming. A dog will let you practice getting it right, and when you do finally get it right, you will know how to treat your partner and be a better dog parent.

For the men who have influenced me in life, either through direct engagements or indirectly through leadership, I ask for your pledge that if I'm not guiding my son through life, you will assume some responsibility to make sure he has every opportunity to live his life to the fullest, with all of the dignity, honor, and respect he earns. And if he's not fulfilling what you believe are my expectations of him, please become involved!

44 Rules to Live By

1. Rule number 1: The most important rule of life.
2. Balance: Live your life for you, and live it to the fullest.
3. If you can understand the history and propensity of man, then you can be the inspiration of change.
4. Please and thank you.
5. Have a mission, purpose, vision, or meaning for your life.
6. Frame, reframe, azimuth checks.
7. 4Fs: Family, Faith, Finance, Fun.
8. Think globally, plan strategically, act locally; be consistent.
9. Fail forward; measure learning.
10. Self-reflect; take a long mirror view.
11. Failure to plan is a planned failure.
12. Understand propensity.
13. Be flexible/adaptable.
14. Standards: Slow is smooth and smooth is fast; 91% is an A, 61% is passing.
15. Take initiative; don't wait to be told what to do.
16. Eye contact: Gain, maintain, and communicate.
17. Judge fairly, although you will be judged and it won't be fair.
18. Be careful when you show your teeth; many people are afraid of the angry Black man.
19. Take chances.
20. Your reputation matters; let it be yours.
21. Network, develop connections, be the connector.
22. Set priorities: routine, urgent, leisure, emergency.
23. Get comfortable being uncomfortable.
24. Seize the day; create opportunities.

25. Be honest with yourself and others; know when to tell the truth.
26. REST.
27. Love yourself, love your partner, be transparent.
28. Listen to what people say, pay attention to what they don't.
29. Listen empathetically, to understand.
30. Don't argue with a fool. Learn when you are foolish.
31. Safeguard trust and guard privileged information.
32. Develop loyalty circles; align values with relationships.
33. Cultivate reciprocating relationships; know the difference between use and abuse.
34. Respect women.
35. Travel. Explore the world and see what you read about.
36. Invest in Self.
37. Plan for tomorrow, live for the day.
38. Define YOUR success.
39. Escalation of action: Diplomacy first, then knuckle up!
40. Shortcuts.
41. 8th TLP and the operations process.
42. Be independent.
43. Maintain your toolkit.
44. Understand.

1. The Most Important Rule of Life.

The first rule of life is for you to determine the "what" that gives you strength, courage, and conviction to believe in yourself to accomplish your life's goals, to chase down your dreams, and be the best you that you can be. No one can decide this for you. I can only give you the foundation. Others will mentor you, employers will steer you, friends will persuade you, your spirit will guide you, but it is you and only you who makes this decision. A person's history shapes and creates the person. Your history will have an effect on how you view life, just as my history has made me who I am and shapes how I view issues in our society.

As an officer in the Army, I often struggled with my own identity. As a young man approaching adulthood, my motivations were to get out of the hood. I despised my community because it seemed my people were stagnant and content with their current situation, despite unfavorable conditions. The Woodlawn neighborhood was full of drug dealers, hustlers, and gangsters, but also some saints. I remember leaving Chicago thinking, "I hate this place and I'm never going back." It would be a decade before I returned, and even today, I feel like an outsider because I never got comfortable with the coldness and callousness of Chicago.

I consciously left behind most artifacts of my past. When I changed my environment, I adjusted nearly everything about me— my clothes, diction, music, and friends—and disconnected from family because I was blazing a whole new path for myself. The reality is, I left one uncomfortable environment for one that was much more uncomfortable—hostile, in fact. I wouldn't disagree with many people who could characterize my new identity as Oreo-ish. I wanted to fit in the environment of my choice, which I saw as the path to success.

As a new student to the University of Arkansas in Fayetteville, I was greeted with so much newness, progressive, forward-thinking Black students, liberal and conservative organizations, professional fraternities, and diverse demographics of women who were as curious about me as I was about them. As a commissioned officer, protocols, manuals, and social and professional norms based primarily on white conservative Christian values would be the greatest influencers to my personality, plus a whole new demographic of people who held stereotypes about my identity, professional competencies, and intelligence.

Throughout life, people will put a person into a category because it is easy to see that person as part of a whole, good or bad, rather than a part of the whole. Acceptance or rejection is based on whether you meet a group's or society's expectations. It wasn't until I got back into a Black community that I felt truly comfortable. I had the privilege of teaching JROTC for a couple of years in KC's underfunded, underresourced, and underconcerned Central High School, and it was the most rewarding venture to spend every day with beautiful Black children. I finally found my identity, and I'm comfortable with it.

2. Balance - Live Your Life for You, And Live It to The Fullest.

I have a friend who comes from a very long line of military service. Members of his family have fought in every military expedition since the founding of the country. He believed he had no choice but to join the service, which he did, and was very successful. He served, and now his son continues the family's legacy of service. I find that honorable. Soldiering came easy to me. I was athletic, had great endurance and speed, and was strong, intelligent, and articulate, thanks to some rebranding. These attributes, combined with an aggressive personality, caught the attention of my commanders. They were impressed and groomed me for increased responsibilities and assigned me more difficult tasks. It would be decades before I realized that with every challenge accepted and accomplished, I needed more and more pats on the head. I was working hard to dispel stereotypes and make my bosses happy.

I had the realest conversation ever with my white senior officer, battalion commander, and career mentor when I was a company commander in Hawaii. This commander, who would readminister my oaths of office for my promotions to lieutenant colonel and colonel and preside over my retirement ceremony, conducted my annual evaluation counseling. At that time, my company had the best metrics of any company in the brigade. Most of the other company commanders would have agreed. My commander rated me number 1 out of 5 in the battalion and suggested to his commander that I was number 1 out of 30-something in the brigade.

As my battalion commander was leaving the brigade commander's office, he walked by my office and closed the door, and we opened a couple of beers out of my fridge. Before he revealed the document to me, he asked, "Lex, do you know the difference between a good officer and a good Black officer?" Without pause, I replied, "Yes, for a Black officer to be good, he has to outperform nearly all of his peers; to be one of the best, you have to outperform all." I was rated number 2 in the brigade. At some point in my history, probably during my time as a second lieutenant or maybe even in my childhood, I began to work and live my life to make others proud of me. I didn't fully recognize that the people I needed to make proud were already proud of me—my family!

Live your life to the fullest. Enjoy all there is to enjoy in life, and know when enough is enough. Create measures of learning, checkpoints, waypoints, traffic signals, whatever you want to call them—something that helps you to explicitly communicate those thresholds with the people who are important to you, so they understand your motivations and constraints. Be comfortable with your choices and always travel with a parachute, because some will resent you for not letting them control every aspect of your life.

Understand what is important to you and prioritize energy to those aspects of your life that reciprocate equitably. Your life may never be in perfect equilibrium with the things you *have* to do and the things you *want* to do, but you have to pursue balance, achieve it, and then maintain it. Categorize tasks. *Urgent* tasks must get done right now before any other. *Mandatory* tasks must get done by a specific time (daily, weekly, monthly, etc.) before you are satisfied that the job is done correctly. *Routine or REST* tasks—read, eat, sleep, think—are standard things that keep the engine running. Finally, *emergency situation* tasks are for things that you can't plan when they will occur or how bad they will be; you just know a tragedy will occur.

I've seen all kinds of philosophies about saving money for emergency situations: up to six months' salary, at least $100,000 in cash, liquid assets, etc., etc., etc. Saving some money for unexpected but expected contingencies is important, but even more critical is having a plan and sharing that plan with those who are important to you.

A very unfortunate training accident occurred when I was a company commander, and one of my soldiers died as a result. What made the incident worse is that the soldier did not have his affairs in order. He did not inform his mother or his wife of his wishes, which really didn't go well with his baby's mother's expectations. It was a real shitshow at the memorial when we tried to honor the soldier's life. Unexpected tragedies will occur and will cause people to become distracted with grief, but a plan—even a loose plan—that is shared allows others to help support you and allows you to support others.

I knew that my presence as a Black man in authority could inspire and uplift other minorities who had been marginalized and overlooked. It wasn't my mission to empower others under my command, to mentor and guide them towards their own paths of success. My mentoring of other minorities evolved until I became a field grade officer and took on the official role as mentor. But even with my accomplishments and leadership, I faced the constant battle against stereotypes and prejudice. I had to work twice as hard to prove my worth, to dispel the assumptions that came with my race. It was exhausting, and sometimes I let it defeat me.

I built fellowship with other Black officers, building a network of allies who believed in each other's potential and pushed each other to be the best version of ourselves. Although we seldom were in the same units, our faith in each other pushed us forward, even in the face of adversity.

Although late in life, I realized that my true power came from embracing my authenticity. Society may try to diminish my presence, but I refuse to shrink or dim my light. I am proud of who I am, and I will not apologize for it. I have learned that it is not my responsibility to make others comfortable with my existence. I am here to live my truth, to break down barriers, and to inspire others to do the same. By embracing my identity and standing tall.

3. If You Can Understand the History and Propensity of Man, Then You Can Be the Inspiration of Change.

There's a debate in the Army about which is the best leadership school. Some may argue for Ranger School, a very physically demanding course that relies on leaders to be resilient and persevere through physical, mental, emotional, and sometimes spiritual challenges. Others may argue that the School for Advanced Military Studies is the best because it challenges officers to think deeply about conventional military wisdom and dogma. I would argue that both are equally challenging and demanding, and both offer significant competencies. Since not everyone attends both of these schools, those who do are most likely to be better leaders due to the timing and development stages of their career, as well as their aptitude and attitude, which they developed while attending these schools. History has proved that key leaders at every level who have attended these schools will demonstrate the greatest potential to continue to lead at the highest levels of our military.

If selected, the average infantry lieutenant will go through Ranger School in his early 20s and SAMS in his early 30s. According to a leading gerontologist, the human body matures physically around 27. Gerontologists also suggest that the early to mid-30s is the age of acceptance of one's social and economic positioning.

After studying the military accomplishments of the "firsts" such as Richard "Flip" Wilson, Benjamin O. Davis Jr., and Colin Powell, I deduced that in order for me to increase my potential for success, I needed to take the toughest assignments, work harder than my peers, and tolerate being the "only" in a group of peers and seniors, with all the stresses that accompany success. Because their history was captured somewhere, I gained a perspective and lessons about mistakes and good decisions to make. That does not mean I didn't make mistakes, because I did and was rightfully punished—not fairly, but rightfully. When confronted, I admitted fault, took ownership, and was punished.

The sun sets, fall approaches, the tides roll, and the moon orbits with consistency every 28 days and has done so since humans kept records. These records allow scientists, geologists, farmers, and artists to predict future actions with a high degree of accuracy. Several years ago, friends traveled to KC because we were expected to see a once-in-a-lifetime eclipse. People booked their hotels months in advance, but days before the actual eclipse, weather forecasters presented a very nasty outlook for clouds and rain, with a very low possibility of witnessing the full effect of the eclipse. Some people took the predictions and positioned themselves to get remarkable photos of the once-in-a-lifetime occurrence, which anyone could have experienced. When we take the same approach to education and personal development and prepare ourselves for the future, we can create our successes. Or we can remain rigid in our thought process and blame changes in conditions or new facts for not attaining success.

Studying history allows us to learn from the mistakes and successes of those who came before us. It allows us to gain valuable insights into human behavior, societal patterns, and the consequences of certain actions. By understanding the historical context in which certain events or trends occurred, we can make more informed decisions in the present and future.

For example, studying the Civil Rights Movement in the United States provides insights into the strategies and tactics used to fight for equality and social justice, which can be applied to the struggles many organizations and nations face today, of diversity, equity, and inclusion. History also helps us develop empathy and understanding towards different cultures, societies, and individuals. By learning about the experiences and perspectives of people from different time periods and regions, we can break down stereotypes and prejudices and foster a more inclusive and tolerant society.

Furthermore, history helps us to critically analyze information and develop our own informed opinions. By studying multiple sources and interpretations of historical events, we can learn to identify biases, evaluate evidence, and make well-rounded judgments. This is particularly important in today's era of misinformation, where governments are literally rewriting history, identifying the benefits Blacks received because of slavery.

When you apply your understanding of history and place yourself and your skills at the intersection where opportunities meet, then you will have greater opportunities to achieve your goals. Fortunately, the internet is providing excellent resources for entrepreneurs and innovators to create and collaborate with.

4. Please And Thank You.

Cliches such as "It's hard for a person to say no to you if they know you and even harder to say know if they like you," "Kill 'em with kindness," and "It's easier to catch flies with honey than vinegar" are all examples of the powers of being courteous. Being polite and humble will create opportunities you might not have anticipated. Be humble and never talk down to people. Be especially conscious when people work for you or are doing work for you. Display respect to elders even if they are taking your order at a fast-food restaurant. People who talk down to others need to feel superior. They have personality flaws.

Since I came from such humble beginnings, it was uncomfortable at times when soldiers treated me like I was special. Somewhere along the years, people started listening when I spoke. By the time I was a battalion commander, people actually expected wisdom from me all the time. When I walked into the building at the beginning of the day, a soldier would jump to the position of attention and at the top of her lungs yell, "ATTENTION," and remain there until I said, "Carry on." With that much power and reaffirmation, it is easy to see how many of the military's senior leaders, athletes, actors, and other highly successful individuals fall prey to Bathsheba Syndrome. I did.

The story of David and Bathsheba is indeed a well-known biblical tale that showcases the consequences of immorality. King David, a man after God's own heart, falls into temptation and commits adultery with Bathsheba, the wife of his top general. In order to cover up his sin, David arranges for the general to be killed in battle. However, this act does not go unnoticed by God, who sends the prophet Nathan to confront David and pronounce judgment upon him.

Through Nathan's rebuke, David realizes the gravity of his actions and repents before God. Although he receives forgiveness, the consequences of his sin remain. The child born out of the adulterous relationship dies, and David's household is plagued by various troubles. The story of David and Bathsheba serves as a cautionary tale, highlighting the destructive power of power. It reminds us of the importance of accountability, integrity, and humility in our personal lives and leadership positions.

Treat each person you meet with dignity and respect. People don't have to respect you as long as they are not disrespecting you. Not every negative engagement needs to be responded to. Some things you have to let go.

Just recently I visited Kacie and Baby Bella, who live three hours south of KC in Rogers, Arkansas. It's typically an easy trip down Highway 71 with very few disruptions, and the countryside is beautifully decorated with rolling hills, farms, and rivers. This visit I rode my '08 Street Glide, Ozzy Mo. I used to be able to ride until the 5-gallon tank was near empty (over 200 miles). But now that I'm 50, I pretty much need to pee about every hour.

The first town I stopped in was Rich Hill, Missouri. I didn't need gas, so I stopped in McD's for a sausage egg McMuffin, a restroom, and coffee. While eating my meal leaning on my bike, a police officer pulled up within 10 feet of me. I'm sure he had run my plates. While sitting there, I was on a FaceTime call. I guess the cop got annoyed that I was not moving, so he interrupted my conversation to ask where I was going. To the best of my recall, here is the conversation.

Officer: Morning sir, where you headed?

Me: (To Theo) Hold on a second, a cop is asking me questions. Excuse me, what did you say, sir? (Unfortunately, 2-year-olds don't understand when you tell them to hold on.)

Officer: You didn't hear me asking you a question? Do you speak English?

Me: (To Theo) Hold on, hold on, let me call you back. (To the officer) Sorry sir, I was on the phone. How can I help you?

Officer: Where you headed?

Me: I'm riding down to Arkansas. Is there something you need from me?

Officer: You got your license and registration on you?

Me: I do, and it's buried in the saddlebags, but can I ask why you need to see it? I'm just sitting here.

Officer: I'm just checking to see if you are all right.

Me: Sir, I'm just taking a break and grabbing a quick snack, and I'm almost done.

Officer: Take your time, it's a hot one. You be safe.

Me: Yes, sir, you too.

Officer: What does that mean?

Me: Sir, I was just wishing you a great day like you gestured to me.

The officer said nothing as he drove slowly away and parked across the street. I threw the remainder of the sandwich and the hash brown away, downed as much of my coffee as I could stand, hopped on my bike, and left. The officer followed me for half a mile until I got on the highway.

In general, I respond to everyone respectfully by using sir or ma'am, regardless of age. But this fat fucker with a gun shook me. He made me nervous and uncomfortable because I was disadvantaged by whatever the "facts" were and I knew they would not be in my favor. For a moment, I thought I would be the next unarmed Black man killed in America because a cop-initiated contact and feared for his life. After nearly 30 years in the military, I'm not shaken easily. I hate that I allowed someone else to control and terrorize me. I felt like in the middle of America, my truth would never be told.

For the next hour, I trembled over what could have happened if the cop had exited his car. Would any of the regulars having their normal Sunday morning coffee have felt obligated to speak or act on my behalf, or would they have supported their local law enforcement? However, I was going to the introduction of my granddaughter, so I forced positive thoughts into my head. I was on two wheels, the weather was great, and after all, nothing really bad happened, right?

Just south of Joplin, Missouri, I stopped for gas. After filling up, I pushed my bike from under the overhang so someone else could access the pump. I found a pack of cigarettes in my dash bag; they were about nine months old, but I lit one up anyway. Three pulls into it, another cop pulled up and was the friendliest Harley-Davidson enthusiast ever. He blocked my bike, got out, and asked questions about me, my bike, where I was going, where I'm from, how long I've been riding, etc. Maybe he was achieving the same effect as the other cop, but he did it in such a way that I didn't feel threatened. Still, when he first approached me, I was guarded because of the previous engagement just an hour ago.

Officer: Hey buddy, nice bike. That's not a factory paint job, is it?

Me: Do you mind if I grab my registration and insurance out of the saddlebags?

Officer: What for, pushing your motorcycle out of the way? Nah man, I just want to take a look at your ride.

Me: I'm just a little nervous [at this point, very nervous] because I just had a not-so-friendly conversation with another cop. I suffer from a little PTSD, and with everything going on I'm quietly freaking the fuck out internally, and it manifest itself as uncontrollable shaking.

Officer: OK, OK, no worries. Yeah, are you always this nervous?

Me: Nope, never, no. I am aware of what I look like from the outside, like I'm hiding something, but no! Not when I'm in my element. And this old-ass cigarette isn't helping.

Officer: Want one? I have a pack of Camels.

The officer pulled his Camels from his pocket, grabbed one, lit it up, then passed the pack to me.

Officer: [Long exhale] That is a sweet ride. Have you been to Sturgis? [Etc. etc., etc., more bike talk.]

Officer: Sorry, let me get this thing out of your way. You probably feel like I got you trapped.

Me: Well, you do!

Officer: I guess I do. Have a great day!

Me: Thanks for the smoke. Have a great day as well, sir.

The next morning, before I left Baby Bella, I made sure I wouldn't have to pee for three hours by not drinking water or coffee. I filled my bike up in Rogers because I know my 5-gallon tank at 45 mpg would get me all the way home or very close, depending on the wind and weather. It was a rough ride back without coffee and without stopping. Thirty minutes outside of Kansas City, I got caught in a storm but didn't stop and got home with about a gallon of gas left.

Keeping it 100% may be real to you, but it may NOT open doors for you as well. Keeping it 100% in this particular situation could have been tragic with the first officer. The reality is, the plates on my bike were technically expired, because I had renewed them online three days before and had a temporary emailed copy of the legit license. The license was sitting in my mailbox when I got home.

5. Have A Mission, Purpose, Vision, Or Meaning for Your Life.

What will be the narrative of your life? How will your family, friends, acquaintances, and peers describe your life? My approach to having a meaning in life wasn't intentional, planned, or coordinated through the efforts of invested parents and the community. I came about my mission because I didn't want to be stranded in Woodlawn, feeling hopeless that the world would continue to progress without me. Without having a strong purpose in life, I adapted the Army's purpose and culture because it had a structure and a desired end state. I did not have much of a purpose until I went into the Army, and although I have no regrets, I wish I had had my own purpose to marry and align with the Army's purpose and mission. After joining the Army, I progressed through life for the next 15 years without giving much thought to why I existed.

I like to compare religious communities' responsibility and processes in indoctrinating values and meaning into their followers, which influences their selection of partners, careers, and lifestyles based upon the church's values. Well, the Army is very effective in indoctrination too, with rituals, rites of passage, elite communities, and beyond-reproach leadership.

When you select a person as a mentor, leader, or adviser, make sure that person has morals and values greater than your own—definitely not one who consistently demonstrates disregard for diversity, lacks tolerance, and spits divisive and hateful rhetoric. Know evil and avoid it, but if necessary, arm yourself with knowledge, pen, and—if necessary—sword. Not every fight needs to be fought, but when hate disrupts and threatens you, your life, and your family and friends, attacks your values, or forces you into a demeaning way of life, you must fight! Fighting is a discipline. Be disciplined while fighting.

I've spent some quality time with some quality people over my life, but lately, the single thing that is the most gratifying and consistent for me is the first hug! The first hug from my children is the most rewarding—wet binky, drool, bad breath...bring it! They continuously connect and reconnect me to my purpose in life. The first hug from my siblings, because despite the length of time, I always feel like it has been way too long since I last saw them... priceless! That weird, awkward hug from dog parents who really think they are as simpatico with their dog as I am with mine. The first hug from my favorite cousin, then my other favorite cousin, then the other other favorite cousin, well, that type of love is... empowering! The first hugs from my brunch/life crew and getting deep, I mean deep, and even deeper, then diving in a little bit deeper in conversations...that is epic!

The departing hug after meeting someone new and feeling, "I'm glad I gave this person a chance because I really like this person..." vibing! The hug from the friend who doesn't let you take a knee on your morals... expectedly! That warrior's hug from a veteran, old, new, grunt, pogue, or POS... that's the truth! Unexpectedly, out of nowhere, a random hug from a baby with beautiful, fat cheeks and electrifying eyes...nostalgic! Being hugged by my daughter, and then by my granddaughter... mission accomplished!

6. Frame, Reframe, Azimuth Checks.

Throughout your life's journey, be prepared for success, setbacks, more successes, shocks, and failures. How you frame your life and develop your life's plan will define who you are and how you solve personal and professional problems. Some life changes—planned and unplanned, prepared and unprepared—will cause you to reframe what you have already determined as your path. When—not if—this happens, you should be prepared to make changes or adjust your plan for additional people and different spaces, places, and locations.

I define any situation that requires decisions as a problem. This problem can be simple, complicated, or complex. My Army evaluators all revered my ability to isolate and solve problems as my greatest competency. I was successful because I led teams that framed problems and applied appropriate solutions, and when the situation or the facts changed, we quickly reframed the problem with the new knowledge and adjusted our tactics.

Simple problems have simple solutions and tend to be easily solved by applying known techniques. Complicated problems tend to be harder to solve because they typically have multiple systems that support their ability to stay a problem. Solving these requires an ability to deconstruct a framed problem in order to apply solutions to part or multiple parts of the system. Complex problems tend to remain unsolved because we typically don't frame the problem correctly, or else we determine that the problem is too difficult to solve right now. Complex problems are more challenging to isolate because they involve multiple interconnected networks of complex systems.

At this point in my life, I view all decisions through the lens of a physical structure, The House of Neal, to help me understand how the problem is to be solved. My family is my foundation, and they will come first. The foundation is holding up three columns: faith, finance, and fun. These hold up the House of Neal.

I am extremely fortunate that Nele's mom kept me connected with Nele despite extended combat deployments, training rotations, continental separations, and our complicated relationship. Nele's mom understood my childhood, and although she and I didn't work out, she made the connection happen because I shared with her the importance of being a father to my child. The rest of the frame is the vertical columns that support my mission in life.

There have been times when significant events and shocks caused me to re-evaluate my life, to reframe. The critical questions when reframing were: "Is this what I am meant to do with my life? Do I need this (thing, person, pet, job, investment, hobby, etc.) right now in my life?" Reframing doesn't mean I change my values or my beliefs; it means I achieve a deeper understanding or another understanding of my values as they compare and contrast with where I am in my life and my plan for my life. Periodically, I took realistic assessments of myself—azimuth checks—and asked, "Am I going in the right direction? Have I achieved what I planned to achieve? If not, what do I need to do differently or in addition to what I am already doing?"

When I was faced with the complicated decision of whether to continue working in the Kansas City Public Schools, I reluctantly decided to pass on teaching for five years and thus become eligible for a second retirement. I framed the problem like this:

How do I support the future of my family in pursuit of fulfilling our full potential as citizens of the United States, protected by rights, in our fair Kansas City by maintaining and building our current network of family/friends with mutually supportive relationships, sustaining current financial investments and increasing financial net worth while enjoying all life has to offer?

My solution was easy after I framed the problem by isolating the things that were relevant to the situation: my offspring, the belief in giving back to the community, being financially secure, and enjoying life. Teaching is very rewarding work, but I didn't enjoy working really hard with a bunch of distractions to have a positive impact on one or two students. Faith Wise, I believe in teaching, but I found other ways to volunteer to help those in need. Economically, I made more money working from home as a consultant. I decided that I would not return to teaching and subsequently became a partner in a very lucrative business venture.

7. Four Fs: Family, Faith, Finance, Fun.

The 4Fs help me to define and prioritize the things that are important to me daily. The House of Neal considers the Family the foundation supported by three pillars: Faith, Finances, and Fun. Most of the time, I'm successful in connecting with my family, either daily through direct contact or FaceTime or weekly phone calls. Family always comes first. Family is siblings, parents, grandparents, cousins, aunts, and uncles. However, you will experience some friends who are closer than family because of shared experience. Your spouse is and should be your closest family. There should be no space between you and your spouse. Have an approach when it comes to family and closest friends: If it is a reasonable request, then say yes. Give freely to your family and expect nothing in return.

Faith in a superior being, a spiritual guide, God, etc., has always been a challenge for me. As a child, I spent Sunday morning in Sunday School, afternoons in service, and then dinner at the church. On Wednesday, while my sister went to choir practice, I met with the deacon for the young deacons. As I got older, my questions began to alarm my family and the deacons. Their response was, "Don't ask questions, just believe." I was never satisfied and started my own quest for religious understanding. I know this broke my mom's and my family's hearts, but I don't believe there is a single being controlling the world. It is hard to imagine that Jesus—who I believe was a person—experienced the earth and during his stay didn't openly condemn the institution of slavery. It is even harder for me to imagine that there is an "all knowing, all good" who allows so much bad to happen.

I place faith in myself to find my own balance and seek happiness thoroughly. I believe I will continue to experience happiness because I can create freely, accept people as they are, and have found meaning in my life. I am conscious of how others see me, but do not need their acceptance. All of my needs are met according to Maslow's hierarchy of needs.

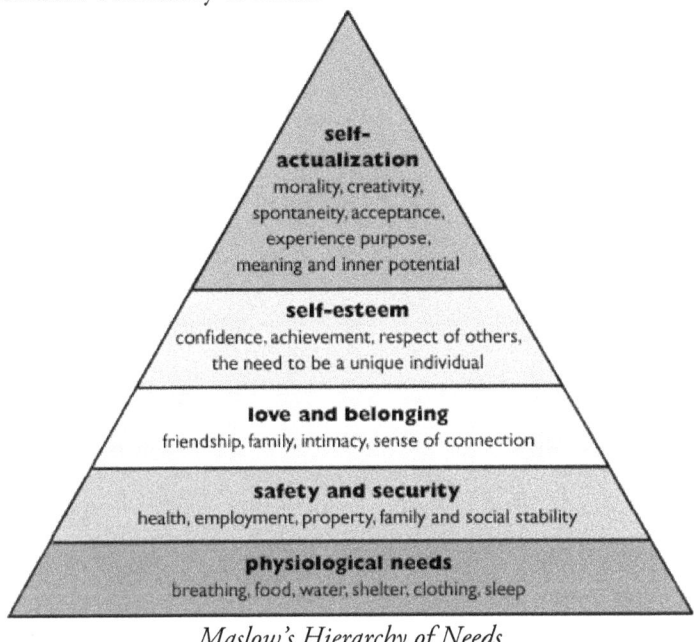

Maslow's Hierarchy of Needs

I am financially secure and have a high credit score, which means I am living the American Dream, which elevated me from one socioeconomic status, out of poverty and welfare, to having transferable wealth for the next generations. As a kid, I watched my mother struggle with money; we never had enough and seldom went without many of the necessities. Living in poverty causes people to go to extremes to feed their families. My mother did, and eventually she was arrested for passing bad checks. As a first-time offender, she was given probation, and her voting rights were taken away. My mother died in August 2008 with about $600 in her account. Being financially secure allows me not to worry about money. Having a high credit score enables me to take advantage of most financial incentives, like a 2.25% mortgage or 0% interest when buying cars.

Unfortunately, the trauma I experienced as a kid still affects me today. I refuse to be a victim of economic depression. I stress about owing money or being late making payments. As soon as a bill hits my mailbox, I pay it. I started investing 10% of my income at 17 years of age and maintained that discipline of paying myself first to this very day. As my status in life changed and I received promotions and pay increases, I adjusted from 10% up to as much as 30% of my salary.

I remember being a Private conducting Payday Activities when you stand in one line to receive your cash pay, then get into the next line to donate to the drill sergeants, then the next line to donate to army's emergency fund for soldiers and families, then the next line to donate to the museum, then eventually the last line where you buy money orders for the rest of your cash before you get in line to pay for a haircut. I thought to myself, if I can survive after donating 30% of my salary, why can't I donate that to ME? I learned to skip the donation lines.

I remember teaching financial literacy to my students at Central HS. We discussed the risks and rewards of credit and the importance of developing budgets. Many of my 18-year-old students already had negative credit history due to parents neglecting loans or unpaid utilities that were opened under the child's Social Security number. These kids financial future was fucked before they got started.

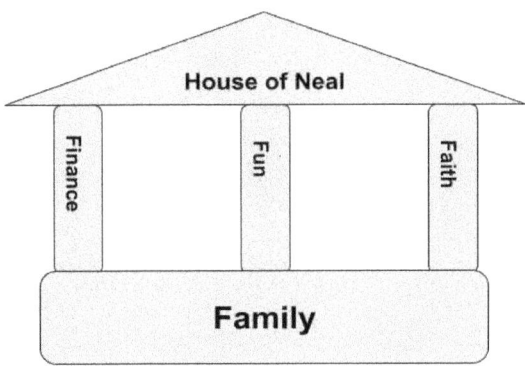

Fun is defined as living my life freely to the fullest extent of happiness possible. Fun includes vacations, dining experiences, adventures, staying healthy, concerts, cultural excursions, and exercising. Deciding to have fun is an algebra problem where the only answers are 'No' or 'Yes,' with caveats, by managing risks. I love riding my motorcycle; it's risky, and there is a greater chance of death if involved in an accident, but I still ride. I never skied before skiing with a bunch of experienced lieutenant buddies in the Austrian Alps. At that time, I was resilient and bounced pretty good going down black-rated slopes. I'm pretty much the bunny slope type of guy now. Almost everything fun has a risk or cost.

I had many exciting, adventurous vacations as a young man. Now my vacations are much more subtle, still some adventures, but not as risky. Actually, the greatest risk I have to consider now is how much the fun thing hurts my body. As a young man, I had to consider:

How much time would it take, and what am I sacrificing to spend time having fun?

How much money will it cost, and what sacrifices will I need to make for fun?

How much time am I taking away from family, or is this about family?

8. Think Globally, Plan Strategically, Act Locally; Be Consistent.

The world is a mysterious place, and it has an even greater mystery if you only hear about it from someone else. When I was a kid, I remember my mom watching Jimmy Carter debate Ronald Reagan on our black and white television. I remember it because there was nothing else on television on Oct. 28, 1980, because of the debate. Why was my mom watching this when most of my neighborhood and family didn't vote because they perceived their votes as not counting? One reason was the potential impact on our neighborhood with Reagan's crime initiative to increase policing in urban neighborhoods. My mom stated that she heard something about how the Republican candidate wanted more "law and order" to combat the extreme violence and drugs in inner cities. About the same time, I began to observe some of the community leaders initiate local movements to improve our neighborhood and to get more young people off the streets and into the communities. Parkway Community Center became a safe place for me and a lot of kids in my neighborhood. Stop and frisk was a way of life for many people of color for the next four decades.

I remember the "Get Out The Vote" campaigns and drives. I remember watching scores of young diverse groups coming through my neighborhood, which in itself was unique, because at this point in my life, the only white people in Woodlawn were some teachers, cops, and a Greek family who moved onto our block. I also remember how scared my mother was for my uncles and the men in her life before the election of Chicago's first Black mayor, Harold Washington, in 1983. My mom, along with most of my neighborhood, believed there was a systematic plan to arrest any Black man walking the streets and detain him until the election results were posted.

As a military officer, I really started paying attention to what was going on in the world because the US military is the most effective, most efficient, and most reliable institution of the executive branch. It always obeys orders and never publicly questions the political masters. The US military has been involved in hundreds of publicly known and named overseas operations since I joined the Army in 1989. Military members are assigned to every embassy and are tied strategically to our nation's interests. Whereas I grew up not caring about the global community, I quickly learned that a lot of the military's efforts are vital to the nation's ability to carry out DIME—diplomacy, information, military, and economics—as campaigns or tactics. As a young officer, I grew up watching Fox News and Headline News. As I matured, I listened to more center of the road CNN, then explored with Al Jazeera, MSNBC, and BBC. I regularly listened to NPR to gain a better understanding of the world.

As a result of the Internet, the world has gotten much smaller. Now, when an overzealous police officer shoots an unarmed Black driver because he fears for his life, the rest of the world knows about it. That action and subsequent wrongful actions that involved super empowered people who took advantage of flaws in our social justice system inspired the Black Lives Matter and Me Too movements. After a school shooting in Florida, a group of teenagers marched on the state capital, demanded gun reform, and got it! Teenagers getting involved at the local level sparked change. Now we need some adults to pick up the football and carry it across the goal line.

It is hard to watch the news during the election season, which starts right before the last election ends, because news agencies broadcast divisive rhetoric to their loyal viewers, who thrive on the luxury of having their favorite anchorperson provide their own biased and self-appointed "honest" presentation of facts. The greatest problem is that we've become so divided that we can't even agree on the facts. I can't believe some of these politicians actually believe what they say to the press to support "alternative facts" and deny empirical data, which can be measured and determined "true." It used to be that CNN was the television station in the middle, the most credible, but now, with all of the alternative facts, CNN is viewed as being on the left. Listen to what stations broadcast (left, right, and the middle), but conduct your analysis of the facts as they relate to you.

When you have that type of awareness of what's going on strategically, you can get involved at the local level. This gives you the option of selecting representation from within your community. What gives your voice, your actions, and your beliefs weight when fighting for what you believe in is when your message and purpose are consistently transparent!

When I was the commander of a basic combat training battalion, my peer commanders and I believed infantrymen were the best trainers; my battle buddy and I were both infantrymen. As part of my in-brief to incoming trainers, I would show preference to infantry but tell all my trainers they were excellent and equally valued. I also expressed my strong commitment to equal and fair treatment of each and every person assigned, which was up to 1,500 people at times. One of my best and senior sergeants made a statement to her supervisor about my apparent preference. She asked her leader not to say anything, but he did. When he made me aware, I immediately called for the sergeant and publicly apologized to her. My actions and words did not match: I lacked transparency and made the psychological correction internally, and began to demonstrate that I did value them equitably for their training abilities and not for their assigned gender or previously assigned function.

It is the dawn of the 2020 election, and the environment is on fire, literally. The West Coast is on fire, the Southeast is being ravaged by hurricanes, and the entire country is suffering from COVID-19 fatigue while political machines continue to divide our nation. Change will not happen because you wish for it; change occurs when people get involved and are inspired by the right reasons or the right people. Get involved in movements that are important to you. Support local organizations and institutions. Get out and meet the people who are running in local elections. Find out what their motivations are and determine if it is something that you can get behind or lead. Find local chapters of national organizations so you can volunteer and donate to effect change at the local level. By supporting local and community organizations, you can help select those leaders. Collectively, when we help to select local leaders, we can support the foundation for state and federal government positions.

Compare and contrast the involvement of parents in education. Parents who are active and involved in their child's education tend to have more influence on school boards. As an educator, I observed that the parents who didn't get involved typically had kids who didn't do well in school. The parents who were involved in the school were also involved at the district level and were able to influence the entire education system.

Consider how many times local police officers have been deemed "fit for duty" after they initiated contact with a person of color, feared for their safety, then shot and killed an unarmed citizen. How is it possible that a person couldn't do the one job they swore to do—to serve and protect—and still retain that job? One of the artifacts from our past that keeps reinforcing this lack of transparency or accountability is that many people in authority positions believe Black people need to be controlled and observed because they are "different" or "not us."

"You know how they are…"

"I'm not prejudiced, I'm just saying…"

"My experience [although very limited] has been…"

Whatever the excuse is that provides the justification to treat people different than them differently.

9. Fail Forward; Measure Learning.

"Man, I could've joined the Army, but…"

"I was a beast in high school; I could have played in the pros if…"

Listen to what people say; pay attention to what they don't. When I hear these phrases from people, I have a visceral response that I tend to conceal. Those phrases typically precede the excuse for why they didn't succeed at something. When you pay attention to the rest of the story, you find out that the person had a desire and may have had talent, but didn't have the courage to fail a few hundred times to achieve success. Frogs are one of the most imperfect creatures in the world. Each frog has the hope that each hop will land on the desired location, but achieving that perfection seldom happens. Still, they precisely arrive at their special lily pad. Just because you don't stick the landing doesn't mean you didn't earn the points by learning to do better.

During the first few minutes of class, I used to eavesdrop on students while taking attendance and getting the class prepared. Monday mornings were especially interesting. I was shocked to know how early young people started smoking weed, drinking alcohol, having sex, and being overexposed to violence. Most of it was big stories, often third or fourth hand and some just bullshit. I also learned that a lot of our young people were parented by television and cell phones. Some students spent the weekend with another set of parents, cousins, or grandparents. I became good at "ear hustlin," as the kids call it, because it gave me an opportunity to understand where my students were and how to deal with some of their behavior and/or learning issues.

To avoid random violence, a lot of my young students would spend countless hours on their favorite game systems over the weekend. On Monday, during current events briefs, students would tell stories of relentless attempts, dramatic ends, conquests, and defeats as they played their favorite video game. Sometimes, kids would spend the entire weekend pursuing perfection of their game. I also found that many of these same students failed to prepare themselves for class, either showing up without the proper tools or being totally exhausted from their home lives.

My first lens that I viewed this particular situation was that my students spent an entire weekend advancing stages in a first-person shooter game or Madden, but refused to spend 30 minutes preparing for school. Which means that most of our students prioritized being successful at video games over an education that may lead to a greater investment in their own futures. Getting good at Fortnite so you can beat your cousin next weekend is not an equal investment in yourself like preparing for the ACT or Common Core evaluations.

I have experienced failures at every stage of my life. Regrettably, in some circumstances, I decided not to allow myself to settle, to be marginal, ordinary, or mediocre, only going as far as what others expected of me. If I allowed others' expectations of me to define me, I would be the statistic for an urban Black man, dead or in jail by the time I reached 25.

Because I gained a purpose in life, I couldn't accept the first, second, or 13th closed door. I refer to these failures as measures of learning, like learning how to advance through the next stage of the gaming system. A failure is one who gives up after trying, or the one who gives up before starting. It is easy not to fail by not trying. If you are afraid of failing, or that if you get it wrong, others will laugh at you, then you are destined not to succeed.

There is a huge difference between failing and being a failure. Failing means you are learning, or at least learning a way not to do something. The failure is the loser who doesn't get back up after getting knocked down. If you are failing, then you are trying. According to Confucius, we obtain wisdom by three methods: first by reflection, which is noblest; second by imitation, which is easiest;

and third by experience, which is the bitterest. Just as it was for me, most young Black men reaching voting age don't have the progressive life experience to compete with their peers, so we learn to imitate until we get the experience. However, we also must reflect on ourselves and our environment to attain knowledge and position ourselves to advance socioeconomically and spiritually.

10. Self-Reflect; Take A Long Mirror View.

Similar to Confucius, I believe you reach that noblest knowledge when you can objectively see yourself in your environment and synthesize how you fit in that environment. This is a lifelong goal of mine. Growing up stuttering made me take a lot of precautions when it came to expressing myself. I absolutely hated reading in public, from third grade through adulthood. Each time I was required to read out loud, I panicked, sweating profusely while blundering over every syllable. Even in that moment, I could see the stress on most adults' faces when I spoke. I could also see the faces of even some of my family, faces filling with excitement as the mockery and laughter began. Stuttering made me withdraw to the safety of my mother and sister. I became dependent on my sister to help me maneuver through life until I could get control over my stuttering.

I'm not sure exactly when I stopped, but it was somewhere between stuttering over every syllable, to every word, to once in a sentence, to – I catch myself sometimes. That transformation started in the 9th grade, and I'm still working on it. When I reflect on the communication journey, I realize that stuttering didn't make me withdraw—how I believed I was being received by others made me withdraw. When I withdrew, I taught myself to speak. I became a more effective communicator, which made me a better leader and ultimately led to a successful career.

It has been my goal to understand the cognitive dissonance between how I see myself, how others see me, and how I truly exist. Since I am self-confident, I know I am not as tall as I feel, I am not a great dancer, and probably not as handsome as I see myself. If I didn't have a lot of self-confidence, then I'm probably not that bad-looking, I'm vertically challenged, and I can keep up a tune for a little while. There were times in my life that I thought, I'm the best, #1, top dog, and had the confidence to say it to another person. That was when I suffered some of the most significant setbacks. If you get to that stage of your life where you are on top of the world and untouchable, then you are living the Bathsheba Syndrome. Conversely, there were points in my life where everything seemed like it wasn't worth the fight, but there was always a better day.

Synthesizing on where you are in this life is essential. Self-reflection allows you to put things into perspective. This analysis creates a narrative of a Venn diagram in which the three circles intersect and overlay each other. The organism where your values and beliefs exist within all three circles defines your true you. From there, you only have to ask yourself: Are you living the life you want, or is life being lived by you?

11. Failure To Plan Is a Planned Failure.

Cliche alert:

"Not all plans survive first contact."

"A plan is only as good as the designer."

"Plans always fail anyway."

Leaving the house without a plan can be fun and exciting, but mostly you waste time and resources and achieve little. The experiences you do achieve are typically the result of luck and circumstance, and rarely is that luck repeated. When I was a kid, adults asked me all the time, "What do you want to be when you grow up?" So, I naturally started asking kids the same question. There is a huge difference in the responses from high school teens from military backgrounds, the KC suburbs, and KC's urban core. For the majority of students, the response is pretty similar—usually something to do with being successful, sports, medicine, law, science, etc.

Where the divergence occurs is with the males and the follow-up questions. With the non-urban nonminority students, the majority of males have a drive to be successful that is similar to the females, and they more than likely have an idea of how to travel from high school toward their dreams. These students tend to invest in themselves academically, motivated by their successful parents, and plan to excel academically and/or athletically in high school and then in college, to major in the field that gets them to their desired end state. When I ask urban Black male students the same questions, their answers are to be entertainers or athletes, as well as other successful businessmen, but they do not understand the pathway to their dreams. Some even believe lightning could strike again in their favor and land them in the NBA like LeBron.

Out of over 20 million high school students in over 26,000 high schools, less than 2% of those students actually make it into any professional sport. I feel torn explaining the statistics to these young boys of color, who in many ways place a huge bet on luck and not enough on education. I explain that their pathway to the pros is through succeeding in high school and then college, and if you do extremely well, you may make it to the pros. But not planning or preparing yourself is planning to be a failure. Failing and learning is an investments in self.

There's a gigantic difference between failing and being a failure. Failing is a way of learning, and as long as you learn not to make the same mistake, then you are learning another way not to do something. I've heard the saying that you don't get good at something until you've done it 10,000 times. Can you imagine the number of shots Steph attempted before he got good, then the number of good shots he made before he got great? Each missed shot provided feedback—more wrist, less backspin, more arch. Each made-shot—confidence!

Being a failure is different. You failed at something and stopped, or even worse, you didn't even make an attempt. As a teacher, I would ask for volunteers to solve a problem. The students who were not afraid of getting it wrong and being embarrassed were the ones who eventually got it right. The students who were afraid of being laughed at often refused to try or half-heartedly tried so as not to show effort; they were the failures. Those students were setting themselves up for a lifetime of settling for what others allow them to have. They failed to dream and failed to fail, and more than likely, their lives will be filled with statements like, "I could've been…," "When I was…," "I wish when I was younger, I had…," suggesting they missed their opportunities for success.

How many times have you heard that not everybody is meant to go to college? My response is: Why not?! The purpose of college isn't to teach you the right answers to the questions; college teaches you how to solve problems. After my brother, Cleveland, turned 30, we had a discussion about how he feels he is now better equipped to solve problems than his peers who are now starting off in the same career field. I assessed that his four years as a prison guard have given him problem-solving exposure and thus confidence. I explained it to him this way:

"High school teaches you how to solve problems. Although it is important to get the right answers, it is essential that students demonstrate they understand the process to solve the problem. Remember the stress when you were called to the board to solve a2 + b2 = c2, then exponentially the problems became harder to solve as the years progressed? College continues the known problem-solving repetition to increase the likelihood that when you see an unknown problem, you can creatively solve that problem."

It is my belief that a college graduate's persistent exposure to solving problems over time provides more opportunities for cognitive growth. Students quickly amass capabilities that make them valuable assets to global corporations. Those students expand their abilities to think critically about problems, communicate effectively, and collaborate with others to solve problems creatively.

Cleveland didn't plan on being a prison guard. When I asked him if this was his future, he replied with a firm no. After high school, he tried college full-time, part-time, then no-time. He worked a few jobs, then four years ago, he started his current job. Cleveland is now in the self-reflection process and deciding what his future will be. I believe he and the typical college graduate are cognitively aged about the same through their unique professional challenges of solving problems they've experienced. I believe the biggest difference when comparing the two paths is systemic: one had a plan and a support system.

Most of us would agree that we would never attempt to travel across the US without having the essential tools such as transportation, funds, a map, a GPS, routes, a compass, and a support system. Why are so many of us willing to risk so much more by traveling through life without having a plan? The plan starts with a dream. Dream big! If a man can walk on the moon and Barack Obama can be the first Black president, and if any other person can do it, then you can accomplish it as well. Plans should begin with a narrative that describes the current situation, continue with effects-related waypoints, and then end with a desired outcome.

12. Understand Propensity.

"If you can understand the history and propensity of man, then you can be the inspiration of change." I wrote this quote when I was in the School of Advanced Military Studies, while my class studied Eastern philosophy about propensity. I love the quote by Orison Swett Marden:

"Whatever you do, don't discourage your dreaming propensity. Your heart's desires are not empty vaporings. They foreshadow possible realities. Man was made to aspire, to look upward."

I feel a significant population of African Americans is resigned to letting the politicians figure out the world because there is nothing they think they can do to influence anything outside their direct control. As a teacher, I made it part of my curriculum to cover current events during the first few minutes of class: at least one topic from local, state, national, or international news that students could receive participation credit for. Initially, when I started, students were reluctant to speak up. The majority of the events mentioned revolved around crime in the neighborhood, especially on Mondays, and very little about what occurred outside the communities. I did find that the students who were class and school leaders were more aware of news outside their direct neighborhoods. By the end of the school year, more than half of my students caught on and started watching or listening to the news. Or, probably more accurately, searching the web before or during class.

The moral of the story about propensity is: If you do nothing to effect change, then your expectation of change should be exactly that—nothing, for you or for your community. When I was a young lieutenant, my first platoon sergeant used to tell me before every operation or training event, "See yourself, see the enemy, see the terrain." He offered this advice because, as the leader, he wanted to make sure I made the best decisions to keep our platoon alive while we were deployed. As I matured through Army leadership positions, the concepts regarding propensity evolved as well, from "stay situationally aware" and "stay alert, stay alive" to situational understanding, which communicated clearly more than "something happened" to understanding how or why something happened. As I left the Army, I adopted the cognitive hierarchy model, which describes the entire process from collecting data to gaining knowledge superiority. Through this cognitive process and gaining knowledge superiority, leaders are equipped to make informed decisions with predictable effects on the organization (self), solve the problem (enemy), and create positive and sustaining effects on the environment (terrain).

The most important step in the military decision-making process, otherwise known as MDMP, is step 2, mission analysis. As one of the chiefs of mission command for the Army's Mission Command Training Program, my principal observation on why organizations fail was (a) commanders rely too much on their own intuition to make decisions and (b) staff relies too heavily on the commander's intuition without providing him or her the necessary tools. With commanders' vast experience in comparison with their staff, they typically make decisions based on having seen this scenario before or based on military history studies. The staff who do very little to process data, analyze information, and understand the situation, bias-confirms the commander's decision without improving the commander's understanding of the situation. The only consistent outcome of this type of planning is that the staff is always behind the commander's decision cycle, thus failing to provide knowledge superiority to the commanders—sometimes they've already had it or obtained it on their own. It's not that commanders are flawless and have impeccable intuition. The success of operations, regardless of planning, is driven by the sheer determination of American soldiers to win.

When you understand that certain actions will occur regardless of intervention, and when you can position yourself at an intersection to apply resources, you can effect a desired outcome. For example, if I were a high school sophomore with a strong desire to go to college, then I would take AP classes, receive and conduct tutoring, take SAT/ACT preparation courses, and assist administrators with paperwork for extra credit during college application and graduation season.

13. Be Flexible/Adaptable.

I wish I could say that I am a great planner and every operation or vacation went according to plan. But I can say that through self-reflection, I gained an understanding of myself, my life's purpose, and mission, and I was able to map out my life by setting goals as they related to me and weave the important aspects of my life while living up to the Army's standards. I created decision points that mattered to me and my family, which helped me to understand when criteria had been met, informing me that it was time for me to change course. I got there not because I was a skillful life planner; I was fortunate to have some great mentors. Being adaptive allowed me to reap the benefits of "luck." Being aware allowed me to see changes as they occurred. Being adaptable allowed me to change course when the environment changed and the rules changed.

Chris Grant will hate this story, but when I was a battalion commander and he was my command sergeant major, I would periodically go out fucking off, or OFO. ChiSM—short for Chris, my friend, my command sergeant major, my right hand— would inform me that he would tell the troops that I had an appointment. I told him that I wanted the formation to know that I was taking some personal time, and they too should take some personal time. ChiSM won a few times, but I won some other times on those arguments.

I think it is important to plan some OFO time in your life. Some people refer to that as vacation or downtime. It is impossible to give 100% all the time and every day. Take another little journey with me. Imagine your human body is a beautiful one-of-a-kind special automobile, and you were to drive it from Chicago to San Francisco. For my former students, yes, another math problem. Some may think that just over 2,100 miles, the speed limit averages 75, this great car can easily do 90 mph, I can make it in about a day.

Let's say you successfully make the John Candy Cannonball Run to San Francisco in less than 24 hours without an accident or ticket, or sleep. What did you accomplish? What shape will you be in once you get there? What did you see? What was your experience? You spent 24 hours in a stressed environment, probably artificially alert, you probably permanently degraded the abilities of the automobile, and you will be useless for a significant amount of time once you arrive.

The reality is that if you were driving in excess of the speed limit for such a long time, the greater the odds are that you will have an accident that will stall or end the trip, or you will receive a ticket that will stall and add additional expenses to the trip. It is not feasible to believe that every street light, dense traffic, road construction, random animal crossing, weather, or every other environmental concern will go in your favor. There will be attractions and distractions that take your attention away, people who are interesting and you want to spend more time getting to know, and external and internal issues that cause delays. You can't keep your guard up all the time, which is why every combative sport has breaks. Cars have fuel capacity limits and speed maximums, roads have speed limits, workplaces have policies, governments have laws—all designed to prevent systems from overloading. Tragedies, deaths, and accidents are a part of life; most of the time, we don't know when they will happen, we just know they will. There will be events in your life that you can't necessarily plan for, but your plans should be flexible enough that when these tragedies, shocks, or good fortune occur, you have the ability to stay guided and adapt to a new course if necessary.

14. Standards - Slow Is Smooth and Smooth Is Fast; 91% Is An A, 61% Is Passing.

Most cars, like humans, have an optimum efficient operating speed; let's call it a marathon pace. If you are a runner, you know you can't run a 50-kilometer marathon as you run a 100-meter dash or 400-meter relay. Some people have greater capabilities than others, and if you are lucky enough to be talented and gifted, you will probably exceed most standards. On October 12, 2019, Eliud Kipchoge ran a marathon in 1:59:40, setting a world record. This means he averaged greater than 13 miles per hour for 26.2 miles. In my prime, I ran 6 miles per hour but for only 3 miles. Comparing yourself to others can be helpful to gain an understanding of your competencies. Forcing yourself to pursue someone else's exceptional accomplishments can cause unnecessary mental health risks with unforeseeable tertiary results.

Understanding established or external standards and combining those with your self-directed standards allows you to put things into perspective and prioritize accordingly. Not everything in life requires you to give 100%. Some things may be very important to others but carry no weight with you at all. Your priorities must be conscious decisions, especially if you decide to place a personal priority above your boss' or supervisor's priorities. If you are willing to change a supervisor's priority, you have to accept responsibility for your actions with equal enthusiasm.

After getting out in the world and experiencing some success, I found men I respected and latched on to them as a mentee. When these mentors wrote documents or articles, I read them intently, wrote down their insights, made mental notes, and added them to my briefcase for future reference. I wanted to experience their successes. Without taking into consideration how close they stood at the starting line, I set their standards for myself. In almost every comparable situation, I experienced measurable success to their standard. Those mentors expressed pride in my performance and demonstrable potential for future success. Through their mentorship, they groomed me and positioned me to accept increased levels of responsibility.

15. Take Initiative; Don't Wait to Be Told What to Do.

One of the key elements of my success was that I didn't wait for supervisors to tell me what to do or give me priorities. I believe that when people are young, they harbor some lethargic behaviors; when this is combined with little to no professional or work experience, people tend to wait for someone to tell them what the right thing is. Sometimes, leaders or supervisors get busy and fail to issue priorities to their subordinates. As a result, nothing gets done while their staff waits to be told to do the right thing.

Look at this situation from a supervisor's perspective. He was caught up in a meeting that lasted an hour longer than it should have. When he returned, he was disappointed because his team members were waiting to be told what they should have done. Imagine if someone had taken the initiative to at least start preparing to work. Who would that supervisor find of greater value? The workers waiting to be told what to do, or the employee who didn't know what to do but started organizing equipment to begin work? The supervisor just paid many workers' salaries for an hour to do nothing. By finding out what needs to be done and doing it, you make yourself a valuable and reliable asset.

Supervisors of highly effective organizations want their team leaders and members to exercise good initiative, which should be aligned with the organizational values, initiatives, priorities, and mission. As a young officer, I relied heavily on the Army's eight troop-leading procedures as a formal way of demonstrating initiative to my commanders. In step 1, you receive the mission. Step 2 is starting the initiative by issuing some basic guidance to get the organization started moving in the right direction. Steps 4-7 are actions taken before the plan is finalized.

The Army's Eight Troop Leading Procedures

Step 1. Receive the mission
Step 2. Issue a warning order
Step 3. Make a tentative plan
Step 4. Start the necessary movement
Step 5. Reconnoiter
Step 6. Complete the plan
Step 7. Issue the complete order
Step 8. Supervise, inspect, rehearse

I think it would be hard to effectively measure the outcome of an initiative without the benefit of hindsight. It is equally important to do the right things as well as not to do the wrong things. Throughout my military career, I've heard the saying, "Good initiative but bad judgment." I believe young Black men can avoid the pitfalls of exercising bad judgment by synthesizing the US Army's mission command philosophy with characteristics of a global organization. Every global organization has driving principles for guiding its success; at least four can be agreed upon by all. Global organizations need critical thinkers, effective communicators, and responsible people who can collaborate internationally and creatively solve problems.

*"The philosophy of **mission command** is guided by six interdependent **principles**: build cohesive teams through mutual trust, create shared understanding, provide a clear commander's intent, exercise disciplined initiative, use **mission** orders, and accept prudent risk."* [1]

---

[1]https://www.army.mil/article/179942/applying_mission_comman d_to_overcome_challenges

Before I filled out an application or submitted a resume, I researched the organization. I gained some perspective on the leadership, the mission, and key performance margins and developed questions for the interviewers. I wanted to make sure that when I spoke to the person across from the table, she would be impressed by my homework and my interest in her organization. As a supervisor, when I hired people, I was impressed by the applicants who did their own research.

The US Army has been a great place for me to learn and has taught me some excellent skills that have aided me in every success I've experienced. Some of the best tools the Army provided me were some shortcuts to helping me get organized, gain an understanding of situations, and exercise prudent initiative. The troop leading procedures and the tenets of mission command facilitate a leader to organize, gain an understanding, and apply the four characteristics of global leadership: critical thinking, effective collaboration, creative problem solving, and effective communications.

16. Eye Contact: Gain, Maintain, And Communicate.

Most of us can agree with scientists who believe our relationships begin with eye contact. Whether we are passing someone on the street or making a financial transaction, once we realize that our eyes have connected, we start to communicate. An effective method to demonstrate respect for yourself and for the person you are communicating with is to look that person directly in their eyes. Once you gain that eye contact, you should maintain it (but not in a creepy way) and use it to help communicate your message more effectively.

My experience leads me to believe I should always open a known positive relationship with endearing eye contact to communicate my strong desire to maintain that relationship. Whereas with unknown persons, I initiate the conversations with softer gazes to show interest, but not too much—that could be creepy. With known relationships that are adversarial or aggressive, I initiate with shorter direct eye contact to demonstrate I'm firm and will not back down. Gaining eye contact at the onset or before a conversation begins allows you to set preconditions as you communicate your intentions. This allows you to assess the level of interest and how your communication may be received. According to a lot of social psychologists, specifically ones who research the psychology of eye contact:

"Participants had more insight into their own emotional reactions (which were measured objectively through the galvanic skin response) after they'd made eye contact with a face. "Our results support the view

that human adults' bodily awareness becomes more acute when they are subjected to another's gaze," the researchers said.[2]

Public speaking equals **ANXIETY** for me. The mere idea of standing up in front of dozens or hundreds freaked me out then and still freaks me out now. But in my profession, I had to give briefings to senior public and military national and international leaders as well as my own soldiers. I don't believe I will ever be comfortable with speaking to people in large forums, but when I do, I know that in order for me to effectively communicate with the audience, whether it's one person or a hundred, I have to make eye contact with some, if not all, for them to pick up what I'm putting down. If there are decision-makers or an individual, then those are the persons with whom I have to maintain healthy eye contact to influence my preferred course of action.

When I briefed larger groups, I consistently looked into the individuals' eyes for indicators that the briefing was going well: Am I sinking, is the material boring, or has the decision already been made? Those indicators fed into my decision to continue as planned or to alter the brief.

My experience as a high school teacher and as a soldier and a big brother of two young Black men for 30 years is that most of our African American young men either do not make eye contact, which is seen as insincere or shifty, or are overaggressive in eye contact, which can be perceived as threatening. Avoiding eye contact is a learned behavior. When I compiled Dr. Joy DeGruy's book, *Post Traumatic Slave Syndrome*, with my own experience and multiple readings about nonverbal communication, I synthesized that teaching healthy eye contact and relationships is something our male role models should do for our young men.

---

[2]https://www.insider.com/eye-contact-powerful-2017-3

61

17. Judge Fairly, Although You Will Be Judged and It Won't Be Fair.

"You can't do what they do, Booboo." We live in a society where we easily determine that thousands of white officers were found to be "in the line of duty… justified because they feared for their lives, or had the right to shoot because of a deadly threat" after killing unarmed Black men. I remember being in the army and hearing peers say, "…this was never a problem before Obama was elected…" or "…had he just followed the law, he wouldn't have been shot." I even had a company commander post on Facebook that Trayvon Martin was shot by "…a good controlled pair…" while we were deployed in Afghanistan. He happened to command the majority of our Black Soldiers at the time. He took down the post after I confronted him about it and suggested he take it down before offending the 300-plus soldiers under his command.

Earlier, I said I feel that the mistakes I made in the Army that I was punished for, I deserved the punishment. It just seems that I happened to be at the intersection of: Something bad happened, and this time it has to be dealt with. If you take a look at the prosecution rates for ethnic groups, both civilian and military, you will see that in both situations, people of color are prosecuted at higher rates than their Caucasian equivalents. I've been in organizations where certain less-than-honorable behaviors were organizationally acceptable, unenforced, or just politely not talked about. I was in one of those organizations in which the commander was known throughout the formation to engage in extramarital affairs with subordinates. In a study published by Social Science Quarterly, "Ethnicity Effects on Sentence Outcomes in Large Urban Courts: Comparisons Among White, Black, and Hispanic Defendants," Stephen Demuth and Darrell Steffensmeier concluded:

"Hispanic defendants are sentenced more similarly to black defendants than white defendants. Both black and Hispanic defendants tend to receive harsher sentences than white defendants. Also, ethnicity effects are the largest in the sentencing of drug offenders, whereas race effects are largest in the sentencing of property offenders. Furthermore, the present study demonstrates that the failure to consider defendants' ethnicity in comparing black-white sentence outcomes is likely to result in findings that misrepresent black-white differences."

When you are in a position of influence or power, you will be presented with ethical situations that will challenge your moral decision-making. I had a senior leader who was paranoid and believed everyone was out to get him. He intentionally set traps to test the loyalty of the members of his organization. In one situation, he forced me to lie in public and tell the senior leaders of the organization that I was a failure. He created many scenarios where, if I told the truth, I would have made public disparaging remarks about a senior commander. What a horrible little man! He successfully found discrepancies in all of my actions and openly lied about my character. He eventually was removed from command and drummed out of the Army. Before he did, he crushed my soul from wanting to command at the brigade level.

For about six months, this senior leader, who was selected above his peers to command an active-duty combat brigade, infected the organization with his toxic climate. Although many people suggested my commander harbored racial biases, I could not rule racism out, but neither could I, with any degree of confidence, say he was a racist. Even still, I felt I was judged more harshly than my peers by this particular commander. Traci Burch's article, "Skin Color and the Criminal Justice System: Beyond Black-White Disparities in Sentencing," published in the Journal of Empirical Legal Studies, concluded:

"Among first-time offenders, both the race-only models and race and skin color models estimate that, on average, blacks receive sentences that are 4.25 percent higher than those of whites, even after controlling for legally relevant factors such as the type of crime. However, the skin color model also shows us that this figure hides important intraracial differences in sentence length: while medium- and dark-skinned blacks receive sentences that are about 4.8 percent higher than those of whites, lighter-skinned blacks receive sentences that are not statistically significantly different from those of whites."

The best advice I can give to young men of color: Be prepared to be judged differently, but when you are judging, you have to judge fairly. Sometimes it may work out in your favor, but most of the time, being judged is a liability to Black men. Your actions must be transparent and consistent in the sense that those who earn and receive advancements, and when you have to take corrective or disciplinary actions, everyone regardless of gender or ethnicity should receive what they've earned based on your assessment of what you know about the situation and relevant factors that contribute toward the understanding.

18. Be Careful When You Show Your Teeth; Many People Are Afraid of The Angry Black Man.

I remember having a conversation with my mother about the impressive senator from Chicago who was running for president. I told my mother how the cadence in his voice was familiar to that of a Baptist minister. He was tall, dark, handsome, and articulate. He spoke with clear guidance, demonstrating his intelligence and mastery of the English language. He always appeared to be poised and ready to verbally duel with adversaries. He was very selective about showing emotions in public. He knew that if he were to gnash his teeth (like the white man who eventually succeeded him as president), there would be those on the right waiting to portray him as the quintessential evil negro depicted in white nationalist propaganda. Keep in mind, people wanted to impeach him because he wore a tan suit in public, whereas 45 tried to overthrow the government, and people still support and forgive him, or wish his treasonous acts away.

President Barack Obama, like the rest of us, was aware of the double standard of expressing oneself as a Black man. It was so relevant that the popular skit by Key and Peele frequently portrayed a gentleman as the President's "anger translator," depicting a character who could actually say some of the things most people may say in certain situations. Is this reality disguised as fiction? YES!

As a commissioned officer in the United States Army, I was a professional, but at multiple points throughout my career, there were senior officers who discredited my professional opinion because they believed I wasn't qualified to offer an opinion, whereas my Caucasian peers were. I had one supervisor who was just the biggest condescending asshole ever. I was pretty fed up with his dismissive nature and, in a very mature way, confronted him about it. He vehemently denied he harbored any negative feelings toward me, but did state he thought I was intentionally being subversive because I didn't stay in my place. My place is at the table, my place is where my voice carries my message, and my place will not be dictated to me by another man who doesn't respect me or my heritage. Although being removed, fired, or relocated was professionally embarrassing, it felt like someone lifted the weight of the entire world from my chest. I was finally able to breathe, but the damage was done. That was the first time in my military career when I felt the Army was not for me any longer.

19. Take Chances.

I remember when I left for college, my grandfather said, "You'll be back—y'all always come back with your tail between your legs." My stepfather conveyed similar sentiments. I don't recall any of my family being proud that I was off to college; if they were, they didn't express it to me at that time; they merely forecast my failure. For the next three decades, I wondered: What if I had a strong support system—what else could I have accomplished? I was very unprepared for college. My high school experience was sketchy; many of my counselors were more interested in just getting students to stay out of trouble instead of preparing teenagers for life after high school. I didn't have the benefit of parents or older siblings, or cousins who could tell me about college life. I did have one cousin, James Sims, who played football for Nebraska, but in the early '90s, we didn't have Snapchat or Facebook for me to keep up with him. I felt everyone expected me to fail.

I was resilient, and I didn't know it. African Americans are resilient people because throughout our history, we have persevered through slavery, Reconstruction, Jim Crow, the Klan, oppression, segregation, and internal and external violence. All of this contributes to some of our community suffering from what Dr. Joy DeGruy describes as post-traumatic slave syndrome in her book of the same name. This is also the book I gave my mother two weeks before she died. My key takeaway from the book is that many Blacks adapted survival behaviors resulting from others' belief that they were intellectually and genetically inferior to Caucasians.

Despite an unsupportive family, not having the educational background, and knowing I wasn't ready for college, I arrived at the University of Arkansas' School of Architecture in January 1991. I felt inferior because my only real experience in life was about 16 months in the Arkansas Army National Guard, with 6 months of that spent in basic and advanced training. I already started excelling militarily and made a name for myself, demonstrating leadership potential. The education I received from Chicago Vocational and Turrell High Schools didn't prepare me for success or continued education. It was hard, and I struggled with a few classes, drops, withdrawals, and failures. After the first year, my GI Bill wasn't covering my expenses, I wasn't doing "so hot" academically, and going home like my grandfather predicted seemed like the most feasible outcome.

I felt like the world was stacked against me when I asked my mom for some financial help. That was the last time I asked anyone for help. Mom said she had to ask Cleveland, who flat-out said no. I was on my own: no support system, running out of money, and feeling overwhelmed. Instead of going back home, I took summer sessions, applied for financial aid, took out loans, maxed out credit cards, sold blood, worked part-time and full-time, anything I could do not to go back home as a failure. Well, I did it!

The best chance you can ever take is on yourself. But don't rely on luck – place yourself at the intersection of opportunity and skill. Take a chance when you lock eyes on that very attractive person and introduce yourself – maybe that person feels the same about you. Be prepared to express yourself if that person does. The skill is the work you have taken to be your best self.

Sometimes, taking a chance can lead to some amazing adventures. Big Dog met me in Frankfurt while I was on my mid-tour rest and relaxation from Operation Iraqi Freedom in 2005. The day before I reported to the airbase, we went to an Italian restaurant, arriving there near the conclusion of lunch. The family was gracious enough to host us even though they would soon close. Instead of a quick lunch and shoveling out the door, we spent the next 10 hours eating, drinking, and getting to know four generations of the owners' family. This is one of my fondest memories.

20. Your Reputation Matters; Let It Be Yours.

As I started to experience success in the Army, I noticed that people had heard of me through different connections, some personal and some professional. Either way, what people heard about me became their truth. If you have a reputation for getting things done, for being effective, for being the person who connects others, then people will seek you out for assistance with their projects. Conversely, if you have a reputation for doing the minimum, for not being on time, for not being a team player, then organizations exclude you from processes.

I like to believe that I am pretty open. I feel it is important to be frank with people, because when you are passive, sometimes the message isn't received the way you desired. I've experienced significant setbacks because of my frankness. After a brief but heated discussion with a new acquaintance about religion, a very good friend of mine explained to him, "Lex won't tell you things to make you feel good about yourself. He feels that it is not his responsibility." That was true then, but it was only an excuse to not be responsible for my words if they hurt.

If elements about your life and values are important to you, then you have to be consistent in projecting YOU. You have to be the one in control of your narrative. How you handle yourself in your personal life will have a direct impact on your professional responsibilities. Based on your reputation, people will be eager to support and collaborate with you, or they will avoid you like the plague. Unfortunately, you also have to protect your reputation from slander from others who may harbor envy or jealousy. The best way to protect your reputation is through consistent and reliable behaviors.

Be cautious about trusting peers. As a young lieutenant, I entrusted a fellow platoon leader with some sensitive information about an unauthorized action one of my soldiers performed while in Bosnia. I sought out his advice because he was a little more experienced than I was. I forgot that my fellow lieutenant was my peer and also competed with me for accolades and promotions. I never held the intention of keeping the information from my commander; I merely wanted to know what I should expect when I told the commander. I for sure wasn't expecting the only other African American lieutenant in the battalion of more than 40 lieutenants to jump at the opportunity to snitch when I asked for advice. When I confronted the other lieutenant about breaking trust, he responded, "Sometimes you have to give up a little meat so they don't come for your bones." I didn't understand what the lieutenant meant at the time, but it was very apparent after that incident that the commander had lost trust in me.

It took me proving myself in combat for my commander to begin to trust me again, although I was the same diligent, hard-working officer from the first day. Through deceit, I let another person control the narrative about me and my competence, for which I had to endure extreme hardship to regain trust from my commander. Fast-forwarding a few years, I outperformed that other lieutenant and was accommodated by receiving preferential assignments and sponsorship from the battalion commander, who mentored me throughout my career.

I made several mistakes and learned the hard way. But by learning forward through those mistakes, I grew wiser and stronger. I wrongly assumed that a person who looks like me is like me. I learned that even though people have professional credentials, their intentions aren't always honorable. I learned that relationships matter and how relationships add value in mentorship and sponsorship. I learned that we live in a competitive culture, and competitors tend to shit on the others in order to place themselves in a better position.

To protect your reputation, you have to be consistent and transparent and control your narrative about YOU. People who respect you will tell stories of your competencies and capabilities. Those who envy you or feel like you just don't belong will attempt to tarnish your reputation so they can be viewed more favorably.

21. Network, Develop Connections, Be the Connector.

Your individual value increases with every connection you make and how those connections "connect" through you. People like to be remembered, and if you can recall that person's "remembrance" or identification, whether it's their name, profession, hobby, or sports team, then you can sincerely enable that person to feel important through your connection or feel socially insignificant—if that is your intent. Back in the old days in the Army, officers wore branch insignias on their combat uniforms, which allowed visitors to the headquarters to know whom to approach for specific reasons. For instance, if you wanted your computer fixed, then you'd look for the lieutenant with the flags on his lapel; for logistics, the wagon wheel, for artillery, big cannons, etc. But if you really want to know what's going on, find the NCO with the worst coffee breath. He knows exactly what everyone is doing, and if he doesn't know, he could make two phone calls and know as much as the action officer.

Being a connector is a huge mental and time-consuming burden, but the reward can yield remarkable results when relationships are cultivated. We all have that friend who is the social event coordinator for your crew or family. She knows everyone's schedule and relationship status, and who has money problems. Through her, family vacations, event announcements, small gatherings, and happy hours are coordinated; with this, she has the most control over venues and costs. Imagine being that operations officer who has an understanding of every major plan and awareness of most company projects. You would be able to connect those who need assistance, track changes to projects, direct or redirect resources, and make strong and powerful recommendations and decisions.

Connectors understand people and organizations as a network of systems organized in slightly messy but well-organized Venn diagrams grouped by subject, education, economic level, and, of course, level of cool. Effective connectors in global organizations typically are charismatic masters of the 4 C's (collaborate, communicate, creative, and critical thinkers) and can prove to be of greater value to companies than they realize. They know who parties, who drinks, who sweats, who hits, who influences, and who has the hookup. Connectors are super empowered people whose influence extends well beyond their official duties, organization, or even their organic company.

On the other side of the spectrum are those who say, "I just mind my business and clock out, I stay in my lane," or "That ain't my job." These are all valid comments expressed by those who are not committed to the organization. If you have expressed these sentiments to your coworkers, which means you've inadvertently expressed them to your supervisors, then it will be easy to let you go when the time comes. If you feel that way about your job, then go find a profession. If you feel that way about your profession, find another one. I know finding a job or profession isn't that simple, but your attitude may make those decisions for you. It is easier for a supervisor to work with folks who are committed, who may make some mistakes, or who may take some shortcuts than with the employee who complies and does no more than they were tasked.

Looking back throughout my career, I have been a connector in almost every organization. Some networks and systems that I operated in were stronger than others, but nevertheless, in each situation, being a connector was definitely a career multiplier. I gained significant knowledge about organizational behaviors and expectations, usually faster than my peers, and because I was known as a connector, I usually found myself in more preferred situations than my peers.

22. Set Priorities: Routine, Urgent, Leisure, Emergency.

If everything is important, then nothing is important. If you wait until the last minute to do it, then it only takes a minute to do it. Both of the previous statements are false because some things are definitely more important than others, and here's the reason: Only the individual doing the task really has the option to determine the importance of the task. Understanding and organizing tasks allows you to set priorities, which should determine which tasks or types of tasks take precedence, even if some tasks are considered more or less important to someone else. As a high school teacher, it was interesting to listen to students rationalize their procrastination. Most of them believed they produced a better product if they waited until the last minute to initiate and complete said product. As the teacher, I totally disagreed, and the students' lack of preparation was obvious in grading.

I group tasks into four categories: routine, urgent, leisure, and emergency. Routine tasks are typically things I can do without a lot of thought or preparation—for instance, cleaning tasks, fielding phone calls, and tracking and charting progress reports. Urgent tasks are the things I must do before I can determine I'm done for the day, or tasks that MUST be accomplished by a certain time or as a qualifying condition for another task. Of course, other people, such as a supervisor, spouse, or kids, may influence when and how you consider yourself complete. Leisure tasks are where I see most young people prioritize their time first. If you want to seriously hurt a teen, disconnect their phone from the internet. Most people would be embarrassed by the amount of time they spend on Facebook, Snapchat, Instagram, etc.

The last and most difficult are emergency tasks. Most normal people don't carve out "emergency time" during their day unless it's part of their profession. Emergencies do happen. Family members die, teens wreck cars, wives go into labor, and when these things happen, they take precedence over everything else you have going on at the time. This is when it is important to have a strong network to help you maintain accountability for your responsibilities.

Here's my assessment of some of the typical and actual events when high school students received assignments with reasonable suspense. I've seen it from three sides: as a graduate student, as a high school teacher, and as a parent of a high school student who thought she could manipulate the system.

After not paying attention when the assignment was issued because she was sending a text to her best friend, Robin asked the teacher to go over the assignment again. After going over the assignment again, Robin protests that there isn't enough time to complete the assignment with all of the other work she has due from her other teachers. Robin immediately sends a group text to her network of friends to get them all to protest when each one gets to that teacher throughout the day. After several attempts to get the teacher fired for inappropriate behavior, Robin sends out another group text to get the group together to go over the assignment. The group discusses the assignment and concludes that it's stupid and not worth that many points anyway. Two hours before the project is due, the teacher asks Robin if she is ready to deliver her assignment. Robin immediately goes into protest that her family experienced a family emergency that required her grandmother to use her computer, rendering her "all ready, complete, fully edited, and guaranteed A" assignment lost forever to the click of Granny's little pinky finger. The teacher asks Robin to have her mother give him a call so he can verify the information. Unfortunately, Robin's mom cannot receive calls at work, so Robin will have to recreate the entire assignment from memory. For the next two hours, Robin blows off her teachers and arrives at class late, with an assignment she just pulled out of her butt.

Prioritizing the things that are important to you allows you to achieve or maintain balance. It is very easy to follow someone else's mission and priorities and forget about your own. Sometimes, despite where and how you arrange your priorities, other people or situations will affect your ability to maintain balance. For a few years, when I was either an operations or senior officer running combat command posts in which the majority of my duties required me to respond to emergencies, the emergencies became my routine, and what should have been my routine tasks became my leisure tasks. During those years, the majority of my energy went into my profession, and I failed at almost every personal priority, including being a husband and father. Be cautious about reaching for the stars—it comes at a cost that cannot fully be understood until you are looking back at it in the past.

Routine	Emergency
- Emails, calls - Maintenance and cleaning - Stockpiling and rotating - Health, shower, eat, sleep	- Deaths - Accidents - Pandemics · - Economic situations
Urgent	Leisure
- Boss' tasks - Spouse's tasks - Home tasks, kids, house, car - Relationships	- Facebook, Instagram, Snapchat - Coffee/water cooler breaks - Gaming, solitaire - Dating apps

23. Get Comfortable Being Uncomfortable.

Being the only or the first African American at something or some place is very lonely and sometimes scary. Even in this millennium, there are still people who have very limited and even no interaction with African Americans. I love going back home to my mom's side of the family with all of my cousins and cousins and cousins and more cousins. I slip into this down south type of comfort, my family is around me, I ease up and get comfortable, everybody knows me—ah, home. At home, whether at TT's house or my own, I'm the most comfortable. Being the only means I had to leave what was comfortable. I had to leave home. I was exposed; I didn't have my tribe. It was scary, and I had to stand with others who, unlike me, had been there before…whatever the "before" was. Many of my peers had traveled on airplanes outside of the US and had health insurance. My first time having a full physical: Army. First plane ride: Army. First real paycheck: Army. I was very uncomfortable with the successful life I was about to live because I didn't know what success looked like or that I should expect endless failures that would ultimately build the foundation for success and successfulness.

From childhood all the way through young adulthood, Europe was just a word, Paris was a town, probably a lot like Chicago, but not as cool, the Tigris and Euphrates weren't any different than the Mississippi. Although I studied architectural history, I really couldn't visualize the grandeur of the most amazing architecture that graced the planet, even though I learned about these structures while a student at the University of Arkansas. Before the Army, the world was mostly two-dimensional because I only saw it through pictures, movies, or television. I didn't know anyone who had experienced anything other than the 530 miles of Interstate 55 between Chicago to Memphis.

The cohort of officers I arrived in Germany with as a second lieutenant was a good bunch of officers who were probably more fundamental to my assimilation into the Army than anyone else. They were there for the first time I used my passport, first time skiing, first time at a formal dinner, first time swimming in the sea, first time in a bar fight, first time driving across international borders. They were able to catch me up to what they considered normal life adventures. Although my buddies were there with me, I was still the *only one* many times, and that made me feel uncomfortable, especially when someone claimed something was unaccounted for. I still have a visceral response when I think about the wife who misplaced her purse in her car, saying to me, "Well, Lex, if you know anything about it, then just let us know. You or anybody can just keep the money; we just don't want to deal with getting new licenses or credit cards."

Getting used to someone accusing you or assuming you are a thief isn't a feeling that anyone needs to be comfortable with, but it is part of the collateral damage associated with a young Black man going outside of his neighborhood into the world. When I enlisted in 1989, the Army wasn't as equitable in offering opportunities or protecting minorities or women from harassment, but over the course of my career, that too would change. As a young man, I didn't really have principles to stand up for myself, but I felt some type of relief when the racial jokes were directed at minorities other than Blacks. By the time I was commissioned in the mid-90s, the racial jokes had been replaced with jokes about sex, sexes, and sexuality. Blackophobia was replaced by homophobia, which was then replaced by transphobia.

Success caused me anxiety. Can you imagine doing something so awesome that people expect that same level of awesomeness from you all the time? How much pressure would that be? Although I've never been that awesome, I have been a consistent and reliable top performer who, whenever asked, always said yes. One of the few regrets I have in my life is that I wish, when people asked more of me back then, that I had the self-awareness and intestinal fortitude to say, "NO, I have done enough."

Being out of my comfort zone was and still is uncomfortable. Speaking in public is uncomfortable, but necessary if I want to make a living. But my comfort zone has expanded significantly and now includes many more parts of the world than I ever imagined, and many diverse and interesting people and foods. The challenges of being one of a few or the only one also present opportunities to create new experiences and narratives. Think about success and how you will accept it before the elements of success control you.

24. Seize The Day; Create Opportunities.

One of my mentors advised me that only a fool would ever turn down an opportunity to command. In the Army, that is mostly a true statement, so as a young captain, I sought out opportunities to command and be strategically in the hardest job that offered the greatest potential for future success. When I was chasing those assignments, I understood that if I performed well, I would be one step closer to feeling equal to my peers. I was selected and promoted to the rank of colonel above many of my peers and still chose to retire, regardless of the potential for promotions and accomplishments. Even still, certain members of the Army just could not fathom rewarding me after 28 years, 5 months, and 25 days of service. According to some, I was an embarrassment to the organization. I did not receive a final retirement award because I broke a minor rule, which I was punished for, and even though the Big Army selected and promoted me afterward and approved my retirement, the officers in the middle intervened to make sure I walked away with nothing that would enhance my resume, not even a final evaluation. Woosa!

Why would I leave the Army when the pay is incredible, benefits are outstanding, and I could have guaranteed myself a six-figure income for the rest of my life? OK there are the things called wars and deployments, which suck, but the reality is, it was more probable that I'd be killed in my old neighborhood than in combat situations in the Army. With enough hard work and determination, I could have been a general—the next Colin Powell or one of the other historic African American generals. But instead, I chose to retire. I saw an opportunity to find myself, and that was the most important task!

We all have heard the saying, "Be careful of what you ask for; you may get it." If you are fortunate enough to become a company commander in the Army, you must expect and accept that your life will change. You will work late and nearly every weekend. At some point you may adjust to getting to work really early before anyone else arrives so you don't have to stay as late, but you wind up working late because shit happens. After I had two very successful company commands, I was offered a third. Against my mentor's advice, I declined because I felt like I needed a break from shit happening.

Growing up, I heard the phrase, "A lot of deals are made on the golf course," which may be true, but I closely relate it to being able to put yourself in the right time and the right place with the right people to achieve a desired outcome. That place could be the golf course if that's the culture you're in. Or that place could be the classroom, boardroom, or a 30-second ride on the elevator. It is making sure that if the opportunity presents itself, then you are prepared to take advantage to improve your situation.

The Army taught me to always be prepared by maintaining inventories and understanding potential outcomes of situations. Near the end of May 2020, after months of going through phases of isolation and quarantining, my family was still situated to hold out for several months if needed. (On a side note: 2020 is an asterisk year; we all get to write this one off.) Because of my Army training, my family maintained rotating stocks of supplies. The Army also taught me the value of having a 30-second elevator spiel prepared to give at a moment's notice and to have a packed bugout bag.

My old commander taught the art of the 30-second elevator spiel, or controlling the narrative. He not only taught it, he lived it. On many occasions while we were stationed in Afghanistan, he educated and entertained VIPs. He wouldn't lead in with "This is where you can help me," or "This is how awesome my troops are doing," or simply avoid the visitor or situations like some commanders did. He would open up by acknowledging what his mission was and how specifically his unit was accomplishing the tasks he was assigned. He was able to effectively prime the recipient before providing whatever information that person was seeking. He controlled the narrative and was able to shape how the recipient was able to hear how well his troops were, how awesome his command was, and then get his request for support actually heard.

By the time I was a diplomat working with Israelis, Jordanians, and Palestinians, I had developed my own rendition of the 30-second elevator spiel, which I adapted depending on the audience. As a teacher, I developed spills every day and used them each period, six times a day, five days a week, nine months a year, for two years. Now, as a co-owner of a medical marijuana dispensary, my spill is:

"I am Lex, and I'm one of the owners of Riverside Wellness, a medical marijuana company. After 30 years as a civil servant, as a commissioned officer in the US Army and high school teacher in KC public schools, I fully understand how reluctant many people are about medical marijuana, but as a user, I wish many people understood the medical benefits of medical marijuana as well as some of the risks. I would love to listen to your thoughts and experiences with medical marijuana use."

In less than 30 seconds, I provided a ton of information about me (businessperson), which now gives me a credentialed platform (civil servant, commissioned officer, teacher) and a biased platform (owner and user) to listen from without being confrontational (medical, benefits, risks) and finally opens up conversations to listen objectively (your thoughts/experiences).

Naturally, if I were a college student or potential prospect to a law firm, my pitch would be a lot different but still concise, with appropriate communication to someone you want to have an effect on, over a brief period: who you are, why you are talking to them, and most importantly, how you want them to remember you. Those people may not remember your name, but they should remember how you presented yourself—hopefully the authentic you. Some personalities can use more energy or props because that is how they roll, but others may find themselves failing miserably if they attempt to mimic another's personality.

Have you ever been excited about a movie because you watched a trailer, just to make the determination that the movie sucks during the first 5 minutes? Did you finish that movie? I never have. Your 30-second trailer while riding the elevator with your boss earned you a briefing role during the next quarterly meeting or, in my case, maybe a business deal with a potential cultivator.

I remember the feedback I received from my thesis defense. I was told, "Lex, you really didn't impress the board. You seemed like you knew your information but your presentation just kinda sucked." That was tough to hear, but it was true. After that lesson, I vowed never to be unprepared for a briefing ever again! It wasn't that I was unprepared with the information; I was unprepared to deliver it. I remembered my information, I prepared answers to almost every question I thought could be asked about my subject, and like a robot, my delivery was freeze-dried, rehearsed answers. The first 5 minutes of my movie sucked along with the next 97 minutes, especially when I was asked questions outside of my prepared responses.

To be better prepared to keep the audience, I learned to loosen up after I was prepared. I got to the briefings or meetings early and socialized with the attendees to talk about other things, which actually helped me to put things into perspective and personalize the delivery. So during the first 5 minutes, I made eye contact with someone I spoke with earlier, and without any choreography, I wove those people and our conversations into my delivery. The first 5 minutes have to relate to your audience in order for them to stay for the rest of the movie.

As a young officer in the Army, I kept myself mobile, always ready with my gear packed to deploy, answering the calls for freedom, even at the expense of my family—or more accurately, especially at the expense of my family. I didn't fully understand until I got older that the "bugout bag" wasn't there to seize every opportunity; it was there so that when the right opportunity presented itself, I was ready to go. There's an analogy about an old bull and a young bull that applies to this situation.

Seizing the day or creating opportunities has both a physical and metaphysical aspect for me. Physically, it means having the tools and being prepared, but metaphysically, it means having an understanding of myself and how I exist in my environment. As a young man, I didn't seek to understand how I fit into an environment; I just wanted to pursue success without understanding what effects that would have on me physically or psychologically. The last psychological bugout bag I packed was my exit from the Army: How I fit into the military-industrial complex changed, and every precondition support metric supported the decision to retire.

As a dedicated father, bugout bags now have pet supplies, baby gadgets, toys, doggie toys, special foods, and blow dryers, and sometimes my bags fill up a full-size SUV. Before, when my bags were packed, it was because I was running toward a perceived better situation than my current situation. Eventually, my priorities changed, and the contents included bringing my family. Now, when my bags are packed, it's because my current situation is so much better than trying to figure out a better situation. Now, my family is prepared to deal with adversity and challenges together.

25. Be Honest with Yourself and Others; Know When to Tell the Truth.

It took most of my life for me to be honest with myself. For most of my military career, I adopted the values and beliefs of the senior leaders of the Army. For instance, Army officers are expected to be married Christians, political pundits, and have an opinion on everything. The strength of your relationships depends on people's ability to trust what you tell them. While I was in the School for Advanced Military Studies, I began to question what I believed in. What I realized is that I didn't *believe*; I just adopted others' beliefs and values until I found my own. When I started being honest with myself, I found myself in a different environment where my voice wasn't the only one; I fit in better with liberals than conservatives, which facilitated easier and more effective communication with like-minded people.

After SAMS, I started diverging from the Army, socializing more with people of color and liberal-thinking folks, and it became customary for me to engage in discourse with my conservative military peers. The politeness of conversation changed slightly as I questioned the alignment of American patriotism and Christian beliefs within the mission of the Army. I had great conversations with my assigned chaplains. The best chaplains for my formations were the ones who understood spiritual wellness as an individual's choice and not an organization's identity.

Many of my peers believe that America is the best country in the world because God blessed America, and the Second Amendment is a God-given right. How do you convince someone whose family has served since the beginning of the country that they are wrong or that you don't believe God exists? You don't; sometimes you just let them be. If my opinion or my beliefs will not change the situation, then I keep that opinion, whether fact or not, to myself.

26. REST.

REST is a simple acronym to help keep a balanced mind: read, eat, sleep, think. Read books, newspapers, and magazine articles. Books should challenge you to explore the past, dream of the future, and account for oneself. Please read anything—not just social media and communications written in millennial-driven text language (idk, lol, omw, jk, nfs)—which engages your mental capacity to understand. Reading some texts and social media posts is very challenging for this middle-aged man; most of the time, I just give up because it's too frustrating. When you find a good author, they can describe a scene that will make your body feel the atmosphere of the environment they illustrate for the readers. Read for self-improvement, entertainment, novelty, information, whatever you desire—just read.

Eating is like architecture to me; it serves a function, and it can appeal to other senses as well. Take time to enjoy fine dining. Cook for your friends. Let the dinner table be the place that brings your community together. I'm not the one to tell you to eat any specific diet, but eat healthy; if it doesn't rot or spoil within a reasonable time, then it probably shouldn't go into your body. I remember being a kid and getting government cheese, cereal, and powdered milk. How is it possible for milk to be stabilized until 2023 when it is 1978? Why did our government distribute artificial preservatives with zero nutritional value to impoverished children without healthcare and living in government-subsidized housing? Maybe institutions that are designed to keep certain populations of people, regardless of race, artificially stagnant and preserved in their current socioeconomic environments, remain in the status quo.

Sleep theory will change over time—at least 6 hours, no more than 12 hours, whatever is recommended... go with it. Sleeping alone sucks. Unless it's your profession, never sleep consistently where you need to arm yourself. It's not good sleep, and if you need a weapon, you probably don't need to be there.

Think about global problems and find out how they affect your community. Engage in discourse with people who are like-minded as well as those who are at the opposite end of the spectrum. Empathetically listen to their debate to understand their argument to improve your position. Once you have an understanding, act within your ability to achieve your effect. Enlist others to join your cause by describing the benefits of such actions. Collaborate to broaden the effect, then mass your movement at the decisive point and voila: The Art of War. I just gave you a block of instructions on military planning. Congratulations, Major.

27. Love Yourself, Love Your Partner, Be Transparent.

Having a partner makes life so much better, but having a partner shouldn't be the end state for every date. Not everyone is qualified to be honored by your love and presence. Never undervalue yourself in a relationship. I had a friend who was in an abusive relationship for a decade, physically, emotionally, and psychologically. Despite intervention by her friends and family, she maintained the image that he was all she ever needed. In the beginning, it was like a fairy tale; the man of her dreams was tall, dark, handsome, and a great dancer. Slowly, he became more and more possessive, then abusive, then made unreasonable demands that she relented to.

They shared an open relationship where he was allowed to see other women, but she maintained loyalty to him. He convinced her into *ménages à trois,* where she engaged in actions she would regret. Years later, she would remember feeling demeaned and disrespected, saying, "I only stayed because I didn't respect or value myself." By the end of their relationship, she loved and valued him more than she loved and valued herself. She eventually broke away and is now thriving as a single mother who is teaching her daughter the value of self.

In every relationship, there will be good days and bad days, but there will always be better days. Being transparent with your partner means you are honest from the first date about your intentions. Sometimes, when you are honest about your intentions, a prospective partner may hide ulterior motives. That's a risk you have to determine if you are willing to take. Good luck; sometimes you will get it wrong. OK, most of the time we get it wrong, which is why most people don't marry the first person they kissed.

I believe the biggest mistake we make in relationships is the expectation that the amount of effort or energy that I put into the relationship equals how great my partner should feel for my actions. Early in my adulthood, many people promoted books that suggested men were from different planets than women, which explained the philosophy of the sexes. Then there were the "however many love languages" that explained the philosophy of fulfilling a partner's needs. Here's the solution: There isn't one. Relationships are not machines. The heart and mind are still a mystery that I hope we never find solutions to because that's what makes us crazy, sexy, and cool. Every argument I've ever had in a relationship boils down to these simple disagreements: "I did [x] for you and you didn't even notice," or "Why didn't you think about me when...," or my favorite, "I don't know what more you want me to do." DO NOT put the ownership of expecting your partner to know what you mean on your partner. Good luck figuring out the rest. I'm still failing forward.

I believe we experience emotional and psychological evolution differently, and based upon experiences, we may regress emotionally, whereas others may never reach that maturity. I also don't believe humans mate for life; otherwise, we wouldn't have divorce or stepparents. Now, if you are in a relationship and you re-evaluate it and acknowledge a change in how you feel about your partner, tell them. Share with your partner your needs and keep them informed on your satisfaction with the relationship or where improvements need to be made. When it's time to break away, be decisive, honest, and compassionate, and communicate clearly and deliberately.

28. Listen To What People Say, Pay Attention to What They Don't.

This was the quote I picked up from my mother. As a victim of abuse from my father, my mother was familiar with the post-abuse apology: the promises that it would never happen again and that was the last time that much alcohol would be drunk. Some of the worst leaders that I dealt with in the Army were the ones who were in it for themselves—the legacy officer, the toxic commander, the overzealous I'm-going-to-be-a-general-someday soldier who will do anything to be rated number one over peers. Their actions and words don't match. They are quick to claim credit and talk positively with self-pronouns and equally quick to identify subordinates' fault for failure. Their lexicon is filled with phrases such as "fulfill our destiny," "we were chosen," "God bless," and others that suggest they were chosen to fulfill God's plan. These are people who abuse their positions to create toxic environments for their subordinates because they feel the organization serves to fulfill that leader's legacy.

If you listen to what a toxic leader is saying, you can hear that leader talking about how great he is and how many contributions he's made to the organization. She is a skilled orator and uses meaningful phrases and words to bring people together, like *family values* and *shared hardship*. When things are going well, you can find the proud peacock with his hands on his hips, gloriously self-congratulating. When things are not going as he would like them to go, there is usually someone in his chain of command who is responsible.

I offer this to you as a bit of advice because that toxic leader is normally pretty successful. He's connected fraternally or familially and has a pretty good record of getting things accomplished. You will not change this person, but this person can change how you view

90

yourself. This was one of the hardest lessons I learned as a young major.

If you recognize you are in an organization steered by a toxic leader, then you have several choices to make if conditions are bad enough where you must leave. (1) Can you walk away and maintain your reputation, and can you afford (financially, career, emotionally) to remove yourself? (2) Can you determine how long you need to bear this situation to put yourself into a better situation? (3) Is there anyone above your supervisor to help bring about a better situation?

Paying attention to what people don't say refers to people who walk the walk and not just talk the talk. This applies to oneself as well as others. If you ever get the opportunity to lead others, then your followers will be more likely to be committed to your organization in lieu of being compliant. Compliant followers will do what they are told because they are following the rules. Committed followers will follow the rules and go above and beyond to meet your intent, even in the absence of specified instructions or rules. Committed followers understand you because you are transparent with your words and actions.

29. Listen Empathetically, To Understand.

Have you ever had a heated debate with someone, and you felt like that person was having a totally different conversation because they refused to acknowledge there was another opinion other than theirs? I've had several of these conversations with my teenage daughter. Why does a teenager doing chores equate to slavery and abuse? To my chagrin, my daughter Nele decided to forgo college after high school and move to Germany for her "gap year" and to be closer to her mother and ailing grandmother. Mom and Oma bought her a car to work a part-time job in a city that has one of the most complete public transportation systems, in one of the safest countries in the world. One day, my daughter called to ask for money because the part-time job she works at doesn't pay enough because it is a low-income and non-taxed job.

The conversation pretty much went like this:

"Papa, I just don't have enough money after I get paid. Most of my money goes for gas, car insurance, and a cell phone."

"Well, Nele, what is the problem with your budget?"

"I told you I don't have enough money."

"Money for what? You don't have to pay rent, utilities, or buy food. Where are you spending your money?"

"I don't have a budget because I don't make enough money."

"So, the problem is you don't have a budget."

"Papa, you are not understanding me, I don't have enough money, and I feel like you are punishing me because I didn't go to college."

I was trying to get my daughter to understand that the problem isn't not having enough money, but rather not having a budget and having an expensive lifestyle. Instead of listening to understand what the correct response could have been based on the question I asked, she responded with what she thought was important: "I don't have enough money." The problem my daughter and I had was that she had an agenda with the desired end state of getting financial support so she could continue her lifestyle, whereas I wanted her to understand what her problem was, what actions she needed to take to fix it (i.e., make a budget and adhere to it), what assistance she needed from her parents, and what she would do if she didn't get the assistance. We spoke right past each other for a good 45 minutes as she continued to tearfully convey how much money she poured into her car each month and didn't have enough money to enjoy life like a 19-year-old part-time employee living with her parents should.

Nele stopped talking only to allow me to speak, but she never responded to the context of the conversation. She skillfully took each opportunity to twist the conversation based upon a misspoken word or gesture to martyr herself. These emotional conversations with her make me feel like I'm in the Twilight Zone. The more I try to get her to understand, the more obscure the conversation becomes.

But maybe the person not listening empathetically was me. Maybe if I spent more time listening to her full argument instead of cutting her off, I would have learned there was a budget, but she expressed it poorly. Maybe if I had listened a little longer, she would have come to the conclusion that she needs to make and adhere to a budget. Maybe if she had not met me with such strong resistance when I offered my fatherly advice, she would have received some of my fatherly cash. As I see it, we both missed opportunities because we both failed to listen empathetically to each other.

30. Don't Argue with a Fool. Learn When You Are Foolish.

I've had conversations like the one I held with my daughter with other people, but usually about politics, religion, and other things we are not supposed to discuss in polite public forums. The political situation with 45 and the articles of impeachment presented boundless opportunities for people to prove how stupid they are. I know why the politicians are talking past each other; they have to support their parties and get re-elected, and I'm quite sure they really don't believe all the BS that comes out of their mouths. But I find it ridiculous for laypeople to repeat politicians' and pundits' opinions as matters of fact because it was on CNN or Fox.

I used to enjoy participating in these conversations because they gave me the opportunity to hear different opinions and test my own abilities to engage in debate or discourse. If someone presented a thought that was logical, I would listen, and if applicable, I would accept that they have an opinion that is different but not necessarily wrong. With this new political environment, politics are always being discussed. Now, when I hear someone's half-assed regurgitation of their favorite pundit, I accept that they are stupid and find the fastest way to leave the conversation. I don't feel the necessity to further explain my opinion, values, and beliefs. It'll be a waste of my energy, full stop!

In the past, I believed it was important to express my opinion to someone who was on the opposite end of the spectrum, but I found that I destroyed relationships. I used to debate with folks on social media. What I found is that most people refuse to admit their logic is flawed, their beliefs are flawed, or that they are wrong. In fact, in my experience, most people, especially when they are adamant and have very strong opinions, even when they are wrong, double down on their viewpoints. They support their positions by stating pundit opinions as facts, or are very selective about facts, or use alternative facts and seemingly negate science and logic. And yet they credit the social changes—or, as I call it, evolution—to "wokeness". Woke people are believed to be vile deviant sexual actors, critical race theorists, and an overall decline in the belief in Christianity. Even though I'm not a Christian, I can clearly see that people who are "woke" tend to act more godly than those who say they are conservative Christians.

There's a saying that goes, "Never wrestle with a pig; you will only get dirty and the pig will love it." It is important that you understand when you are arguing with a fool and not allow yourself to be dragged into a situation where you are not having a constructive dialog, discourse, or debate. With every level of accomplishment, you will become more intuitive and confident in your abilities to assess situations and make decisions. If you are not careful, your confidence becomes cockiness and transcends into your dismissal of diversity and input from others. If you find yourself having the strongest opinion or being dismissive of others' opinions because they are stupid, congratulations—you have become the fool.

Have you ever had a conversation with someone that turned into an argument that started like this: "That's not what I said, you are trying to put words in my mouth"? Well, maybe that's not what they said, and maybe the words didn't come out of their mouth, but they definitely expressed what you felt. If you find yourself in this argument, situation, or predicament, leave!

31. Safeguard Trust and Guard Privileged Information.

I like to think that I'm a good friend and a decent professional. I became privileged to information about people, organizations, and situations that most people could not access based on my personal and professional relationships. Even as a closet introvert, I understood the importance of getting to know people and socializing on different levels in order to increase my opportunities for success. Alcohol is the easy button, but there is also golf, bars, cigars, bikes, adrenaline... whatever opens up opportunities for others to develop relationships based on a common interest, fosters intimacies in which some slowly unveil their insecurities with others. It is important to compartmentalize information and protect that privilege of information because when people CAN trust you, people DO trust you. You will never be able to unknow something you know, but if you know better... do better. Be aware that some people will believe you are unethically benefiting from your position and the information you know, and subsequently will align others and make allegations against you. Be aware and be prepared, and your transparency will be your protection.

Protecting sources of information is the equivalent of a legal nondisclosure agreement or your moral agreement between two people. The caveat of this crucial agreement between honorable people is, when someone or something you once trusted has become less than honorable for you, continue to trust! Many of our first experiences with breaching trust were at home, when a close family member told our secret, then later with friends or classmates after someone got caught cheating on a test, then, when we have our significant relationships in love, work, or with our best friends.

When people breach that trust (they will), and when you breach that trust (intentionally or not, you will), then you have to know what to do next. As I look back on past relationships, there was always someone in my corner asking about a small, insignificant thing about the job or person. At that time, I was so in love with the person or the situation that the small thing didn't bother me. I remember having the red flag conversation with my daughters recently. They were so perceptive of me that they saw the red flags in my relationship while I saw small obstacles to overcome. What they saw as red flags, I only saw as small pink things. I thought *I* was supposed to be raising *them*! Which leads to 32.

32. Develop Loyalty Circles; Align Values with Relationships.

One of the hardest obstacles I had to overcome was blending into circles that I had nothing in common with previously. When I arrived at basic training in the summer of 1990, my only exposure to another culture was the Greek neighbor across the street from me in Chicago and the 10 other caucasians and an Asian who talked with a country accent during my senior year at Turrell High School. Basically, I listened to other music and learned to understand the different dialects from the soldiers who represented the many diverse parts of Americans and others who desired to be Americans. I was promoted to platoon guide or assistant platoon guide for the majority of the eight weeks of training. I believe I was promoted because I was able to get the different groups moving in one direction, and that was because I found a way to relate to them by listening empathetically. Also, I was better prepared than the majority of my peers because I had three years of experience through JROTC and another year of experience because I joined the Arkansas National Guard during my senior year of high school.

Periodically, I got fired when the platoon messed up, which was disappointing but also provided me a slight break from being a pseudo-leader. Inevitably, the replacement leaders would get fired, and I was promoted again when the drill sergeants needed to get something done. My fellow leader who got hired and fired with me was another National Guard soldier from Florida. We were Mutt and Jeff; I believe I was both or whichever one the drill sergeant needed at the time. Even when we were fired, the replacements would come to the two of us to help lead the platoon. The drill sergeants still tasked the two of us with the platoon guide's tasks. We were in the circle of trust.

Being in the circle meant that we got to sit in the drill sergeants' office and talk about the platoon and how to motivate them. We got a better understanding of the mission and were able to provide some feedback to the drill sergeants. We also got access to telephones, and all of the lickies and chewies privates weren't supposed to have. The drill sergeants shared more of their personal life stories and how they got to where they were. I learned then that it was good to be on the inside, just as it was good to be on the inside of my grandfather's circle—until I wasn't.

Being on the inside of Army organizations is pretty hard, except when it's easy. I learned at a very young age to chameleon myself into organizations. That's what basic training in the Army is about: taking whatever values and beliefs you grew up with and adapting them to the Army's values and beliefs. Notice that I didn't say *change* the beliefs. For the most part, people are generally good and were generally raised to do good things. If a newcomer's natural behaviors are so far out of line with the Army's values, then that soldier tends to become a "failure to adapt" soldier. And if no one has figured him out at the basic level, some leader at his receiving unit will.

The culture of an organization becomes pretty clear when you arrive. The center of gravity is usually a charismatic leader who has a tight bunch of trusted allies whom he/she talks freely around. Those trusted allies help lead the organization, provide valuable feedback to the leader, and have expanded privileges. The next circle is the loyal workers who want to be in the circle, and although they aren't as privileged, their loyalty is as strong as those in the inner circle. The next circle is those who do their jobs well but don't drink the Kool-Aid. The other circles are collateral to be used, abused, and discarded at will. Those circles contain the transients—the ones whose paperwork gets lost, misplaced, or forgotten about.

With every success, your reputation—street cred—will precede you. In the Army, the street cred was given to you by your last organization and your enduring reputation. For most assignments I received, I asked a supervisor if he knew anything or anyone at the new unit. And if he did, he put in a call for me expressing how great of an officer Lex Neal was. That usually works if your supervisor was OK with you leaving, but when you make the decision to leave an organization prematurely, sometimes supes aren't so happy and put holes in your boat before you get there.

If you don't have the street cred phone call, then you have to earn your way into the circles. I'm an introvert with learned extrovert behaviors, so I'm naturally more of a watch-and-learn than jump-right-in type. As such, it was easy for me to take the time to learn who the movers and shakers were, as well as who the stewards of the organization were. After watching for a while, I began to engage with the players and jockeyed myself inside the circles of trust. I've jumped into a couple of organizations where the inside circles and I didn't have the same values. Those were the organizations that I found myself not in the inside circle but in the "not to be trusted with our secrets" circle. Those organizations are the ones where I prematurely found my next assignment, and the supervisor wasn't very happy about me leaving as well.

The same should be true for all relationships. I have friends, family, coworkers, and neighbors that I appreciate and spend time with. I don't agree with ALL of their behaviors, values, morals, or ethics, but I just know when to leave before that part of them becomes intolerable. When you understand the propensities of people who are important to you, then you create the ability to position yourself somewhere else when the proverbial shit hits the fan. It's not giving up on your buddy or being a buddy fucker; it's knowing when your buddy has fucked you and is about to fuck you over again.

I have a friend—business associate, fellow entrepreneur, and weed guru extraordinaire—who did an exceptional amount of ground-zero work digging into Missouri's proposed medical marijuana program. This cat was spot on: He found the location, gathered the resources, and picked the team. He fully understood the value of having an African American, decorated retired Army officer, high school teacher, and local citizen on the board of directors, which would give preferential treatment to an application for a business license.

33. Cultivate Reciprocating Relationships; Know the Difference Between Use and Abuse.

We all get used to, and we all use others. The difference is when an effect is not being reciprocated in value or kind. Every person you have a relationship with will impact who you are and the person you are becoming. Who we were, are, and will be is a product of whom we touched and who touched us. Not every person should receive equal valuation in your life. You get to choose who is important and whose values contribute the most. Except sometimes we choose poorly. Love makes us stupid! When it's good, that shit is real goooood! But for some reason, when it's bad, we think it's not that bad or it will get better. The reality is, love makes us stupid!

Trust me when I say that with multiple marriages and equal divorces, I've made every mistake possible when it comes to relationships, and I'm trying to get better. Being honest up front is just an excuse to be used later. Sort of like, "But I told you this is how I am" when building a relationship. Or even better at a breakup, "I told you up front that this is who I am, and it's your fault for trying to change me." Understanding the propensity, I found out that when it's good, it keeps getting better, and when it's bad, it keeps getting worse. That is, until you hit unsustainable expectations. Most romantics like me live for the moment in relationships and expect that same energy, but some people become enraptured in their relationship for that moment, and that moment was enough; then they still live happy lives, and have beautiful families, and... Because I have not accomplished this one, I will only advise: Love freely, love totally, and if you outgrow, love again!

34. Respect Women.

Your sisters, mother, niece, aunts, and cousins will give you the advice you need when you need it, but mostly when you haven't asked for it. Listen to their advice, then make the best decision for you. Respecting women means they have equal access and equal opportunities to succeed and fail. I learned to understand myself more after I developed friendships with my exes. The exes have a great way of telling you how fucked up you are, but also the beauty that they saw in you. I consider myself a feminist, but I still have a lot of work to do. Hopefully, we get to grow together on this one.

The Nation is evolving, and more women are taking positions of power and influence. Be prepared for women to lead institutions and businesses at all levels. We as a gender have not been kind to women, just as our nation has not been kind to minorities. The social changes resulting from the movements are giving us a great opportunity to listen to others. Be careful, not every voice needs to be heard or paid attention to. You have to be prepared to protect yourself if you find yourself faced with one of those challenging situations where a woman is taking advantage of you.

Recently, a middle-aged white woman I know from my old neighborhood, my gym, and KC bars called me to see if she could stop by as she drove by my house. We sat on the porch for about 45 minutes with a couple of beverages. She stated she'd AirBnB'd her entire house out and said, "Why don't I stay in your spare bedroom tonight?". I jokingly replied, "How much does an AirBnB run these days?" Then quickly added that she couldn't because I didn't know her that well, and my son will be home early in the morning. She asked to use the bathroom. I showed her where it was.

From outside, I could see my bedroom lights come on, so I went back inside and upstairs to find her looking around. I turned the lights off and directed her back downstairs. She stated she just wanted to look around. On her way through the living room, she sat on the couch and said she was staying. I became frustrated and told her she was no longer a guest in my house and she should leave immediately. Her response was, "...you are abusing me and if you keep this up, I'm calling the police and you will go to jail because you are black." I repeatedly asked her to leave, then demanded. She made silly demands for me to sit on the floor or she'd call the police. She eventually called the police, and while she was on hold, I called the police to report a trespasser. She told the operator that I was a big black man on drugs and she feared for her life.

After waiting calmly for the police, she decided she wanted a cigarette in but I told her she could not smoke in my house. Reluctantly, she walked outside and demanded that I keep the door unlocked. As soon as she was out of the house, I locked the door and waited for the police. Three police officers approached my house from a point where they didn't see them, but I did. They actually startled her. She began to act hysterical.

Two officers, a male and a female, took her off the porch to get her version of the story. I played the videos from my living room and front porch for the third officer over the Bluetooth speaker on the porch so everyone could hear. She looked stooooopid! The officers asked if it was OK for her to leave her truck in my driveway because, according to her, she had drunk too much and was maybe drugged. Flatout NOPE! The officers waited for her to phone a friend to move her truck. The next day, she accidentally texted me to sell drugs. Two days later, she texted me saying, "I am giving you a heads up, I am suing u for the emotional distress damage in a civil lawsuit. I sent the entire audio recording from my visit to my lawyer. He said it was plenty of evidence there alone to support."

That is a level of privilege I can never understand. None of this made sense to me, and I was at a point of disadvantage. I couldn't put my hands on her to throw her out, and every concession led to her making even more ridiculous demands. Be aware of Karens! Unfortunately, as a Black man, the best tool against Karen is a camera.

35. Travel. Explore The World and See What You Read About.

I was so far behind the other architecture students at the University of Arkansas. I remember taking architectural history, and several students added to the professor's lecture by explaining how they had visited these structures on vacation. I was amazed because the only travel I'd done outside of the Army was the stretch of I-55 between Chicago and Turrell, Arkansas. Beach vacations are lovely, but visiting the wonders of the world and historical sites will provide you with much insight when you are studying or having casual conversations with people.

As a young lieutenant stationed in Germany, I got the opportunity to travel A LOT! In the late '90s, the Army was a lot of fun. The month of February was full of three- or four-day weekends because of all the individual presidents' birthdays. We've since consolidated those down to just Presidents Day. Every weekend, my travel companions—other lieutenants from my unit and sister units—would travel through two or three European countries. Traveling to different countries in Europe is pretty similar to traveling between New York City and Washington, D.C. Make travel a part of your future. Plan, save, and make travel a priority. Find travel companions who have the same interests, and keep your crew tight and small. With larger groups, I found we accomplished a lot less due to the different personalities and appreciations of time.

I have traveled to five of the seven continents and nearly all of Europe. I started traveling with Nele when she was very young. At 3, Theo has three stamps in his passport. See the world and be a part of it!

36. Invest In Self.

The strongest investment that I've ever made was the investment in myself. After reading the stories of many successful athletes like Serena Williams and LeBron James, I gained a better understanding of the tons of hours they spent perfecting their craft in order to become the best at their sports. When awards are given to philanthropists, you often hear that you can tell the value of a man by how he uses his money. To the rest of us who aren't financial philanthropists, we value the quality of a person by how they spend their time. I know several very skillful KC musicians who have full-time jobs and still manage to gig for several hours several nights a week. The gigs they play don't pay a lot of money, but performing in front of live audiences gives them the opportunity for repetition and improvement.

If something or someone is worth your time, then invest in being good at that sport, relationship, or profession. I wouldn't recommend pursuing being the best at everything unless you truly want to be the best at everything. But if that is so, then you have to invest and prepare yourself to be the best at everything. Otherwise, you look foolish professing you are the best when you are not. Rather, I would recommend prioritizing the things that are most important and investing the time to get better or strengthen that relationship or skill.

Wanting to be the best at something requires you to position yourself at the intersection of your skill and the probability that your skill will be recognized. Have you ever gone to a street party and viewed the tumblers, like the ones on Beale Street in Memphis? Those athletes are amazing, whipping out multiple backflips, reaching gravity-defying heights, and displaying an overall amazing control over their own bodies. When I see someone with those talents, I always wonder: What happened? The common response when I've inquired into their abilities was, "Well, you know, I could've gone to college on a scholarship, but some bullshit..." Which boils down to a shortcut that landed that person in an unfortunate situation, or, less likely, a series of really unfortunate events that the person had no control over. Can you imagine if someone had identified that talent, and that person had the time and assistance to cultivate that talent, where his talents could have led him?

There are paths to get you to where you need to be in life, but there are no limitations to where you can go. We all have to pass through the gateways, although some with exceptional talents will bypass some of the challenges associated with making it. Only a few are willing to actually work hard to be better than average or pursue being the best at something. The shortcut comes after many repetitions or after enduring some crucible. As you have these experiences, develop a system or a way of doing things that makes your life more efficient and effective so that you have more focused time to be the best version of yourself.

37. Plan for tomorrow, live for the day.

If there is one reason to capture my thoughts in writing, this is it. I plan on being a father and grandfather to my children and grandchildren, but if I'm not around, then at least they will have this document to refer to how I think, how I believe, and how I lived my life. We don't know how much time is left, which is why we spend our time doing the things we have to do and the things that make us whole. I don't remember thinking about being a father when I was young. Never had I ever thought I would live to be half a century old. I also wasn't haunted by the fear that everything would kill me. Now that I'm older, I can see the value of saving and investing money for retirement. I can feel the investment I made in physical fitness and healthy eating habits. I didn't know how much time I was going to have, especially when the odds were that 1 out of every 3 Black boys in Chicago would end up dead or in prison by 22. The odds were against me!

Live your life with principles and to the fullest. My life isn't without turmoil, but last year was the best year of my life, and next year will be the best year of my life. The Army broke me, but it also taught me to recognize resiliency. The students I taught at Central High School are resilient! Setback after letdown after disappointment, these students have endured so much trauma and, unfortunately, expect to endure so much more. But there are some who broke the cycle of disappointment and worked to get themselves into colleges and universities to improve their situations.

Since we don't know how long we have, we must take the time we have and enjoy it. What good is a bunch of money that you can't spend when you're dead? How old do you have to be before you take a real vacation? When will you ever get a chance to ride a horse on the Capitol grounds? Living today and planning for tomorrow means making budgets—a time budget, a financial budget, a hobby budget, and budgets in general. Budgeting yourself allows you to know whether you are receiving a return on your investment.

38. Define YOUR Success.

When I lived on the South Side of Chicago, one of my cousins, who had recently moved there from Ohio, was religiously and politically connected to the Nation of Islam. Because of this, and as a direct benefit of being an outstanding cook, my mother periodically cooked Sunday dinner for Muhammad Ali when he was in town. At the completion of my eighth-grade year, Muhammad Ali signed my graduation book and asked me what I would become. Without hesitation, I said I would become an Army guy or an architect. At 12 years old, I set a path for the rest of my life. But I really didn't! At Chicago Vocational High School, I pursued a major in architectural drafting and was a member of JROTC. I remember my cousin Jasper making fun of me, saying only sissies take ROTC. By the time I graduated from Turrell High School, I was a private second class in the Arkansas Army National Guard. When I attended the University of Arkansas, I pursued a major in architecture, took SROTC, and graduated from the Arkansas Military Academy, but turned down the state's commission in lieu of a federal commission from the Army.

Moms died in August 2008. Whenever we spoke on a deep level, she asked me two questions and made demands. Her first demand, "Tell me your business." Her first question, "Are you happy?" Her second question, which I never answered, "Have you ever killed someone?" In retrospect, I never answered her first question honestly. My business was the Army, and I rarely looked around to see where I was, so I didn't know if I was happy. I wasn't! I'm still trying to figure out how to answer this question. She would always end our conversations by telling me to quit playing Army and build her a house.

My life is full of accolades and accomplishments. In the Army, you are rated on your performance and promoted on your potential. Throughout my career, I was rated number 1 out of 5, 2 out of 28,

3 out of 42, and so on. I've never fallen below the top 15% in any evaluation. I've received lots of medals, plaques, and other gifts from my soldiers, peers, and supervisors. I was a successful career Army officer, but I didn't enjoy the success. With each accomplishment, I felt the need to drive harder. With each evaluation that leveled me up with my peers, I wanted to improve my rating. I didn't know I was succeeding. Sometimes during my evaluation counseling sessions, my supervisors told me how to increase my rating from 3 or 2 or from the top 15% to a better number. When I was rated 1, I was always reminded that 2 was pretty close, and to distinguish myself, I needed to work harder. They concluded with suggestions on how to get promoted to the next rank and how to get to the next command position. This was the life I lived between 1995 and 2018. I wore a smile on my face in public, but not many people knew how hard I struggled to keep up that appearance.

There was nothing happy about my life other than being a father to Nele. I was always under pressure to perform—to be the best! I lived with two phones that never went unanswered; emails were responded to immediately; I sought out every opportunity to engage in conversations with subordinates, superiors, and peers to expand my influence. I didn't sleep well or eat well, but I exercised like a beast, which is probably the reason I'm around to write this shit down.

I didn't identify beforehand what my success was, is, or would be. While I was stationed in Jerusalem from July 2016 to July 2017 as a diplomat for the State Department, I was broken! My behavior led me to be command-directed to see a shrink. That was probably the worst thing the Army did for itself and the best thing for me. The psychiatrist did a lot of sensory modulation during our sessions, but the most effective therapy was getting me to recognize that I didn't need the Army any longer. Although the Army is one of the largest organizations in the world, I outgrew it. I didn't need to be the best of the best of the best; I just needed to be my best self.

39. Escalation Of Action: Diplomacy First, Then Knuckle Up!

If you believe in something, if you love something, if you love someone, if you value a person, place, or thing, then you have to fight to protect them! When people have beliefs and when their convictions are combined with a strong sense of purpose, some people fight and make extreme sacrifices for their beliefs. Fear keeps most people constrained to the status quo. Either they won't fight because they lack intestinal fortitude and the risk of failing is perceived to be too great, or they won't fight back because they perceive their situation will get worse.

Now at 6 feet and 175 pounds, most people can't believe I'm still the runt of the family. Growing up, being the smallest meant I had to learn how to fight. I took a lot of losses, mainly from my family, but then I learned to give them. I remember graduating from high school and only weighing 132 pounds. When I reported for basic training, I was the only private who was allowed to finish his meals because I was too skinny. I took a lot of abuse from my older cousins, especially Ricky and Junior, who were just a couple of years older. I have fond memories of being tied to things, held upside down, tortured, shot with BBs, and pushed into ditches during every summer I spent in Turrell with my cousins and grandfather.

As a small kid and subsequently a thin young man with a penchant for fighting, I was quick to take offense. My community wasn't supportive of my dreams growing up, but I felt surprisingly comfortable in it because it was the shallow end of the pool. Once I left my childhood community, everything was new—new people, new rules, which all scared the shit out of me—and I thought I had jumped into the deep end of the pool. I felt exposed to the world because I wasn't armed with cultural norms, and I made many mistakes. I hid my insecurities behind a facade of aggressiveness until I felt comfortable being me.

I'm not exactly sure when it occurred, but in a prolonged transition sometime between the first and the last deployment, I realized I didn't need to fight every fight. One of my bosses called me a "natural antagonist." Another characterized me as "always on the red team." They generally respected that I was viewing situations from a different approach, but they didn't expect that I was always ON full time. After those comments, it took some self-reflection for me to see that what I wanted was to be respected for my intelligence, and for me, that meant questioning the policies and procedures that had existed for a very long time.

You see, another artifact of my past that I carried for years is fighting. For my cousins and family to respect me, I had to fight. This is a myth perpetuated throughout African American communities because of the tumultuous history of Blacks from slavery through the civil rights movement. My cousins routinely made me fight other boys my age for entertainment. My family still has enforceable rules such as:

If one fights, we all fight.
We don't lose fights, no matter what.
We don't take threats. If someone threatens you, then you have to eliminate them or look over your shoulder for the rest of your life.

I erroneously pursued this strategy for the majority of my career. For "them" to respect me, I needed to show them that I wasn't a pushover—I had to push back. During those 20 years of growth and development, I became more diplomatic. Of course, it helps to be stationed as a diplomat for the U.S. State Department in Jerusalem, the Palestinian Territories, and Israel to really try to hone skills.

At some points in your life, you will have to fight for what you believe in. Sometimes those fights will be due to physical threats, and some of those fights will be existential to your career. When we fight, it is more about *how* we fight. When we fight we fight with intelligence, we fight for education and community development, we fight to change the experience for better for those who follow us, we fight to get and stay in the room where decisions are being made, we fight to lead the committee of change, we fight for our votes to be heard, we fight for what we believe is right—that's our fight.

40. Shortcuts.

Slow is smooth, and smooth is fast. I think Nele still cringes every time she hears me say this. It's what I think when I see someone trying eagerly to put their shoes on without untying them, but eventually, they have to untie and tie them to get them on comfortably. I have an acquaintance who wants to be a millionaire. He portrays himself as a rich guy, buys stuff, and lives lavishly like a millionaire even though he's not even close. I also know a kid who was a legitimate millionaire at 19. I know some shortcuts that got me from one known point to another known point because I had already traveled the long route and learned a better route. A shortcut that gets you to an unknown point isn't a shortcut; it's a guess. Sometimes we guess correctly and win the lottery, but most of the time we waste resources and time. During an ethics class, one of my students expressed to me that it was OK to steal from companies like Target or Apple but not from people you know. I was one of many teachers who caught the same student cheating on exams and assignments. Her propensity to take shortcuts held her back in her freshman and senior years of high school. She eventually graduated with a lot of undeserved assistance from teachers and counselors.

41. 8th TLP And the Operations Process.

I remember the first meeting I sat on as the incoming executive officer to the 3rd Battalion, 66th Armor Regiment. It didn't go well. I remember thinking, "What the fuck did I just get myself involved in?" My outgoing commander at the time was a bit of a mad genius who took what appeared to be random but horrific ass-chewings and orchestrated the most successful battalion command team transition ever. The outgoing commander asked me to come to a meeting and sit at the head table while I was still on leave. I thought I was there to meet the team I would take over in about 10 days. Three minutes into the meeting, the commander became agitated after every slide displayed inaccuracies. He was clearly pissed at the quality of work from the staff. He turned to me, and in front of all the commanders and staff, thundered, "Hey XO, what kind of fucked-up bullshit is this? Get this shit fixed!" as he prematurely walked out of the meeting. As he left the conference room, I released the commanders and told the staff to stand by. When the door closed, we sat back down, and I asked the staff, "What the fuck just happened?" Turns out Big Lou had a penchant for giving ass-chewings. After I spent a couple of hours reviewing the staff's work, I attempted to avoid Big Lou by sneaking past his office, but he called me in. He explained how he wanted the staff to get behind me. He felt that was the most effective way to get the staff and the XO—me—on the same team. I told him I appreciated the effort, but he could've prepared me for that.

Although I learned the importance of the eight troop leading procedures as a teenager in JROTC, I really learned the importance of the 8th TLP as I became a major. To leaders who dismissed their responsibilities by stating, "I told them," I would follow up with questions like, "Did you supervise the task you told them to do?" "Did you inspect the work before, during, and after?" "Did you prepare your team by conducting a rehearsal before the execution?" Usually, the response was no, and I questioned their ability to lead.

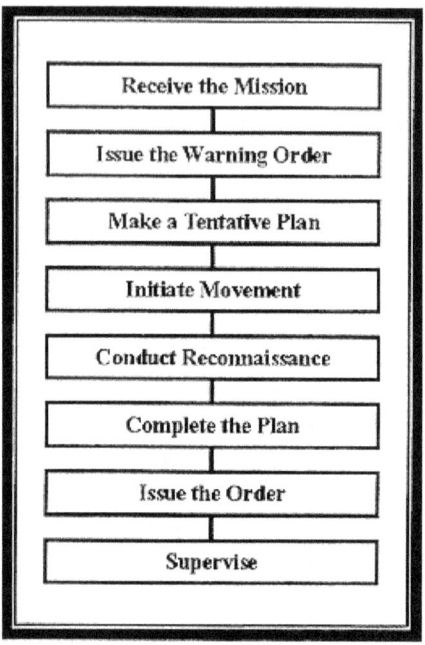

As I matured as an officer, the Army's operations process—plan, prepare, execute, and constant assessments—replaced the 8 TLPs, but the preparation phase is where I found I conducted the 8th TLP. I recently engaged in an online conversation with some buddies about planning. One buddy believed that any plan is better than no plan. Someone else suggested that it's better to wait until to have the right plan. My synthesis from over 30 years of planning experience is to start with a plan that gets you to where you need to be and start moving. The plan will change based on the environment, new information, shocks, catastrophes, and unexpected victories. The plan shouldn't be so rigid that it doesn't allow you to learn from your assessments and make adjustments to the plan when necessary.

The preparation phase is where you start to assemble your resources, conduct your final coordination, and rehearse your plan. That is the point where you identify where your gaps in understanding and resources are, and clearer indications that your plan has a higher probability of success. The preparation phase is where I spent the majority of my time prior to the execution of any operation. Even during this phase, I allowed new relative information to adjust the execution of the plan.

When I use the operations process for a family vacation, I start the planning process with a few texts, emails, and phone calls to coordinate with my kids, then propose a location and timeline. While still in the planning phase, we research and compare hotel costs and amenities, transportation requirements, and fun things to do. After a careful review, we decided on the location, time, and options. Although this could be the most costly part of the trip, I honestly spend relatively small amounts of time actually planning compared with the time I spend preparing. I devote the most amount of time before execution during the preparation phase, when I start checking things off the to-do list. We finalize payments and check to see if the weather is going to be better than in KC. We typically set aside a part of the house to gather the things we want to take with us. This phase can last anywhere from days to weeks. But it ends when we get into the car with all and any pertinent new information being formulated into the execution phase. The execution phase is where we are enjoying or not enjoying our vacation. If we are not, then we make adjustments or cancellations. Those assessments constantly feed into the calculations. When the vacation is over, I'm still making assessments for the next vacation.

When I went into teaching, I used the same principles. I figured that to establish credibility with the students and other teachers, I needed to be prepared. I planned out my lesson plan, gathered the tools I thought would best assist me in teaching, and then rehearsed the delivery of the classes. As a small-business owner, I used the same principles to help our team open our dispensary. As a father, getting my son ready for school, I use the same principles. I wouldn't suggest everyone start using the same principles, but if you don't have a process, then why not?

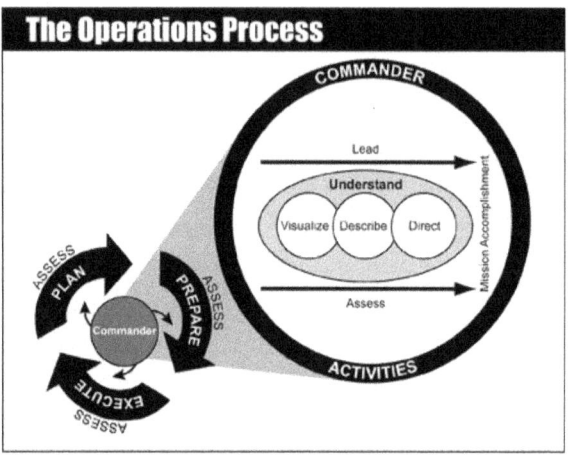

42. Be Independent.

My mother thought it was important for her kids to know how to take care of themselves. She taught my sister and me to cook, clean, do laundry, and maintain our home. Every Saturday morning, I would sneak up and watch cartoons with the volume down because I knew when Moms woke up, it was cleaning time. The blues was the cleaning music of choice for Moms, but she also loved R&B. We spent many weekends scrubbing bathrooms to B.B. King and the Jackson 5. My mother, Sonya, and I would take short singing and dancing breaks that lifted our spirits. By the time I was 21, I had learned to be independent from the Army and my mother.

Even though I started investing early, I didn't have a full understanding of finances. According to Maslow, financial security is just above a basic need, which I now understand is why we never had it growing up. We had the basic necessities…most of the time. I remember one morning waking up to my mother crying because she had begged my grandfather for money. I've heard poor people saying, "Money doesn't make you happy," my whole life. That might be true for some people, but being broke makes you sad, especially when you are struggling with paying the bills or putting food on the table. I remember that for a period of time, we slept in the same room with a space heater. I remember standing in line for government powdered milk and cheese. I remember buying groceries with food stamps. I remember my mother being forced to trade the food stamps at a lesser value for cash in order to pay bills. I remember being teased because I wore my sister's hand-me-downs.

When I talk about budgeting and finances with people I mentor or coach, I get two responses mostly. The mentee who is forward-thinking and doing well with money has a budget. The mentee who is not doing well with money doesn't have a budget. Remember when I asked Nele about a budget, and her response was "I don't make enough money to make a budget"? This is an example of a person stuck in the basic levels of Maslow's hierarchy of needs. Having a budget informs what you can and can't do. Maintaining that budget requires an exceptional amount of discipline.

I have a weird relationship with religion. I spent a lot of time in church growing up with a Southern Baptist mother. By the time I joined the Army, I sought spiritual guidance in Islam, Buddhism, and Catholicism, but was pretty much done with religion, although I still occasionally went to church. As a junior officer, most of the lieutenants went to the same church service as our company and battalion commanders. I prayed publicly with peers and bosses until I was a captain. I stopped because I didn't believe my spiritual beliefs needed to be shared with hundreds and thousands of other people. I don't believe in religion! I believe we have a spirit that needs guidance and reinforcement. I removed a great weight from my soul by gaining and maintaining my spiritual independence to love, live, and believe as I believe.

43. Maintain Your Toolkit.

There's a saying in the Army: "Put that in your tool kit." It means there is something you should write down, commit to memory, and definitely use later. That something could be physical, moral, or psychological; sometimes that something could be someone else's experience. The people who don't make budgets tend to be the same folks who say, "I need to make my own mistakes." This is code for "I really don't care what you are trying to teach me." Learning from someone else's failures is an exceptional tool to keep in your toolkit. One of the best lessons I learned from my mom was watching her work, struggle, and raise two families, then die with less than $1,000 in the bank. Her struggles were real, just like many families from urban and rural environments who have the same experience of being impoverished. I didn't know what my path would be, but as I observed the people in my atmosphere wander through life aimlessly, I started picking up some tools that gave me greater visibility into the future. Throughout my early adulthood, I watched other people make mistakes and tried not to repeat those mistakes. Sometimes I made different mistakes, but never the same mistake twice.

Before smartphones, we had to remember facts, phone numbers, names, addresses, and how to get somewhere without GPS. Smartphones are great resources. Since I was 17 years old, I have carried a notebook with me everywhere. Now I use my phone to take notes, assemble playground and Ikea furniture, get the latest weather forecasts, play games, remind me where I need to be, and just about everything else. Having a smartphone is great, but knowing things is so much better. Get yourself a toolbox with the basics and a few advanced tools, and know how to use them. At some point in your life, you will need to tool around on some things. When you have the option of taking electives, choose some things that can assist you in life—electronics, coding, athletics, woodworking, welding, stuff like that. As you take those electives and learn those tools, add them to your toolkit.

44. Understand.

My last bit of advice for solving complex problems is to seek to understand the system and/or the environment, analyze what you know and determine what you need to know, counter-argue an opposition, then synthesize that knowledge you gained before implementing a solution. I find it best to gather an understanding of the secondary and tertiary effects before making major decisions. Although I haven't done this well, avoid letting a moment determine your life. Sometimes, a single moment or a lapse in judgment may dictate your future and the future of others. Understand that sometimes your actions and words will have unintended effects on others, and you are responsible for that effect. Understand that your happiness is more important than another person's happiness, but if you can compromise, you should understand how the compromise changes the relationship. You can still have a great relationship.

Understanding other people's perspectives makes you empathetic, but you don't have to comply with or condone their perspective to have a conversation. That relationship has boundaries, and you get to set those boundaries. Understand that your lack of action may be complicit in another's transgression, and understand when you must take action. Understand that the world will see you differently than you see yourself, and that's OK because not everyone is special enough for you. Understand that once you have been out in the world, you will see yourself differently. It is hard to go back.

Understand that there are some folks who wish you well in public and pray for your failure in private. Understand that every smiling face is not a friend, but every smile should be friendly. Understand that life is pretty shitty if you allow it to be. Understand your source of power and rejuvenate it when needed. Understand when you need to take a break or muscle through tasks. Set your goals and understand your power and propensity to achieve what you desire. Understand yourself!

Planning and Executing

After spending more than two decades in the US Army, I have learned some very effective ways of planning and executing operations, and I've taken those learned lessons and applied them to business adventures, home buying, family vacations, etc. The most important factor that determines the success of a plan is first identifying what it is that you are attempting to accomplish; this is your mission statement. Once you achieve a clear understanding of the mission, establish your objectives, then develop measures or indicators to determine if and how well you are succeeding in accomplishing your short- and long-term objectives. Throughout the execution of a business plan, conduct periodic assessments; if it becomes necessary, adjust the plan and make course corrections to avoid shocks and predict business success. For a complicated or complex problem, a good business plan starts with understanding.

To gain an understanding of your mission, objectives, and success indicators, you first need to define the parameters that directly influence mission success for the business. For the purposes of this chapter, we will refer to this as "defining the problem." This forces entrepreneurs to refrain from the cliché of "thinking outside the box," but instead challenges them to *create* their own box or the conditions under which a business will flourish. These conditions are based on your mission and what you have chosen to accomplish.

Creating Your Box

Creating your box is the deliberate process of establishing the physical, economical, and psychological constraints and limitations of the business. The box defines what must and must not be done to guarantee success. **Competition.** Who are the real and perceived competitors who may prevent your business from being successful?

Who is the competition and why?

What are the risks of having competition?

Does your competition expose your vulnerabilities?

How do you reduce your own risks and exploit your competition?

Resources available. What resources are on hand or can be acquired easily?

What are the operational requirements?

What are the emergency and contingency requirements?

What does your current credit rating offer you? What are your credit requirements to maintain a functioning business? What risks will you assume with creditors, and if so, how much? How do you prioritize payments to creditors?

What is your economic tolerance?

What is your initial investment?

Time. What are the trends that may have positive and negative effects on this business?

How do seasons affect your business?

What are the earning seasons?

When must you start displaying profits to the investors/lenders/benefactors?

Location. Based on available resources, where can the business achieve the desired results?

What are the physical location requirements?

Does this business exist in cyberspace alone, or is a combination of physical and Internet locations more beneficial?

Environment. What are the environmental factors that can affect sales or services?

What is the physical, seasonal, spiritual, and political terrain?

How does the environment affect the business?

What are the risks, vulnerabilities, capabilities, and requirements of the environment?

Mission Statement

A clear understanding of the mission determines what services or products you will provide. Effectively, the mission statement takes what is implicit in an entrepreneur's head and makes it explicit for others who are associated with or invested in the business. For example, if you were selling a brand of clothing, your mission statement may look like this:

Best Clothing Company imports quality materials from Southeast Asia and distributes to online retail customers and East Coast wholesalers to turn a 40% profit from invested funds each month.

This mission statement is constructed using the Four W's and the How:

Who: Best Clothing Company
What: imports and distributes
Where: East Coast
Why: to turn a 40% profit from invested funds
How: online retail and East Coast wholesalers

This mission statement, in conjunction with the five conditions in which you created your box, sets the foundation for you to develop the plan and envision achievable long- and short-term objectives. As you start answering those five questions, you will start setting the constraints and limitations of your business practices.

Zones of Tolerance

"Zones of tolerance" are the environment, physical, financial, or other personal limitations that you have assessed to fit within your scope of risks—that is, the limits you don't want to exceed. To stay within your identified zones of tolerance, business plan writers should understand seasonal trends and implement measures of learning about the trends and understand what impact they will have. Measures of learning are the real or perceived actions that provide indicators to business owners that their business is trending in desired or undesirable directions. The measures of learning facilitate owners' capability to visualize trends by looking for certain indicators before or as they are occurring. These indicators will enable conscious entrepreneurs to foresee that their assessed limitations are being approached. Assessments and further analysis will determine what course corrections you must implement. Entrepreneurs must avoid making excessive course corrections in which the outcome cannot be anticipated. An understanding of the business's physical, financial, and psychological limitations allows owners to continue to steer the business towards positive trends. If negative trends are realized and the conditions for are established to mitigate the negative trends are established, then recovery from the setbacks can also be anticipated. Business owners must be careful not to extend themselves beyond their constraints and limitations. As the business progresses along positive trajectories, you may desire to revisit your acceptable levels of tolerance. Business owners may wish to increase their levels of acceptable risks to anticipate more profitable successes.

Objectives

The long-term objectives of an organization are envisioned by those who invested in the business. This is how the business owners determine the vision (given the constraints, limitations, and social, economic, and other contributing environmental factors)—by identifying and communicating the realistic objectives of the business. With the understanding of the vision, the planner takes the contributing factors into consideration, projects short-term objectives, and lays out a timeline for those objectives to be reached (see Figure 1).

When carefully developed and analyzed, short-term objectives develop a cause-and-effect relationship with the terminal objective. If interim objective 1 is accomplished and if interim objective 2 is accomplished, that provides the necessary conclusion that the terminal objective will also be accomplished. To accomplish the interim objectives, carefully scrutinize the measures of performance, or MOP. The MOPs are the real and physical actions that are essential in delivering the decisive effects required to meet the interim objectives. Because MOPs are real and physical actions, they are not subject to interpretation as to whether they exist or not.

Contrarily, interim objectives are more subjective and based on the entrepreneur's perception; they are open to interpretation.

Consider this example: Marvin's terminal objective is to get hired for a job. He develops the interim objectives of (1) dress to impress, (2) arrive on time, and (3) interview well. The interim objectives are subject to opinion, but lead Marvin to believe that if these three objectives are accomplished, he will, in fact, get hired for the job. The MOP is the physical actions required to "dress to impress"—maintaining personal hygiene and dressing in a suit and tie. The physical actions required to arrive on time are waking up, having breakfast, and having his route to the office planned in advance. The MOP for interviewing well may be the physical actions of rehearsing his introduction and preparing answers for anticipated questions, practicing his handshake, and standing upright. Although these actions by themselves don't have an individual cause-and-effect relationship on Marvin being hired, collectively they have more of a positive causality, instilling in Marvin the belief that he will be hired.

Trend Identification

Looking at the problem as a whole and creating your box in which your business should exist and thrive, you can expect the life of the business to resemble a wave that cycles through positive and negative trends. These trends are based on physical, economical, and other environmental factors (see Figure 2). The business will have highs and lows depending on environmental factors in the community and economic markets. Throughout the execution of a business plan, you will look for the indicators that lead you to the valid and necessary deductions to predict or otherwise forecast progress. However, it is the planning phase that provides the analysis to determine what indicators will provide those forecasts of future performance. Previously, I discussed the conditions based upon your mission, in which I suggested that you dispose of the cliché of "thinking outside of the box," and rather create your own box. It is the planner's analysis of these conditions by which he or she ascertains when and where potential opportunities will present themselves. The understanding of environmental changes helps the planner not to be deceived by false indicators. Also, during this analysis, the business establishes reasonable conditions to exploit seasonal trends. This analysis provides planners the opportunity to mitigate the risks identified with trends of the seasons, market values, suppliers, and customers.

In risk mitigation, you will conduct an analysis to identify when and where risks will present themselves. Once you understand the risks, you will conduct another level of analysis to determine what effect those risks will have on the business and whether the risks can and should be mitigated. If a risk is too high and cannot be mitigated, the planner goes back to the drawing board to determine if this is, in fact, a suitable, feasible, and acceptable business venture.

Consider, for instance, Best Clothing Company, which provides imported Southeast Asian fabrics that are typically used to make beach and summer textiles for markets along the East Coast. BCC expressed some of the following concerns based on its analysis, which they expect to occur during the fall and winter months:

(a) Northeast US customers tend to reduce their stock levels by 80% from October to March (b) Southeast sales have the potential to remain or even slightly grow during this same period; (c) shipping charges from Southeast Asia increase slightly; (d) energy costs for heating usually increase for the business' physical location.

The company came up with the following risk mitigation measures to offset the Northeast decrease in sales:

Focus sales to customers from South Carolina to Florida; (b) conduct business trips to determine if an opportunity exists to increase distribution to Southeast customers and provide incentives for Northeast customers to increase their stocks for the spring surge (c) consult with Southeast Asian distributors to reduce orders but increase stocks of supplies later in the winter to be prepared for the spring (d) instead of hiring all permanent employees, hire seasonal employees to offset the lower output during the off-season.

Failure to identify trends during the development of the business plan may result in unnecessary changes or even overcorrections. Anticipating second- and third-order effects helps business owners prepare for potential and inevitable situations. Being prepared to take action and thinking through these situations is your way of having an insurance policy for situations that insurance companies don't cover. A good example of failure to identify trends may be:

BKCC failed to identify that the Northeast retailers reduce their stock six months out of the year. The second- and third-order effects are: (a) the company maintained its incoming stocks and ran out of storage space (b) the company maintained all full-time employees throughout the winter months despite not having sufficient work; (c) and the increased cost of shipping caused the company to continue to pay creditors for supplies that they couldn't sell.

Business owners who think through their course corrections are able to prevent "oversteering"—implementing excessive actions to fix a perceived problem. This action usually has a desired short-term effect of fixing the problem, but negatively affects the situation for the long term. This is because oversteering creates shocks to the economic or physical system of the business (see Figure 3).

Generally speaking, shocks are bad and can force a business into colossal failure. Contrarily, it is possible but not likely that a shock can catapult a business into unexpected success. Unexpected successes can be considered the result of a social trend or popular cultural movement that sparks unanticipated purchases of a specific brand or type of material. Neither colossal failure nor unexpected success should be the foundation of a successful business plan. The aware entrepreneur understands the trends and implements the appropriate actions in order to maintain control over the business and forecast an upward trajectory despite recoverable setbacks.

Recoverable setbacks are either physical or financial situations that have trended south of being positive, but are within your expected zone of tolerance. With the application of the appropriate course correction and without expending excessive funding, physical or psychological energy, the business can move its trajectory back into trending positive.

As an analogy, let's say you are a business entrepreneur driving across the country. Before you start your journey, you should determine how much money and fuel you will consume. You may also want to know the best locations to rest and eat. You definitely would want to know which route to take, and you would need to decide how many hours you are able or want to drive in a day. In essence, you want to know where you are going, how you are going to get there, what part of the year to travel, why you are taking the trip, and how you will accomplish it. This is your mission statement for the travel plan. But after you start your trip, you need to make sure that you are traveling along your planned route.

Since you have planned your route carefully, you are prepared for the execution of your trip. You developed waypoints to help you keep track of your progress. If you take a wrong turn, your planned benchmarks assist you in correcting your actions, preventing you from getting too far off course. As you conclude each day's travel, you pull out your map and determine if you are still on target. You conduct preventive maintenance by checking your fluids and tires. You are prepared for environmental changes in case it rains or snows. When you approach an unexpected detour, you quickly determine your next actions.

This analogy should help the future entrepreneur to realize the importance of the analysis that leads to the development of the business plan. A plan that doesn't have benchmarks or measures of learning enables businesses to fail to conduct periodic assessments. Periodic assessments enable a business to determine if it is operating within its constraints and limitations and then make course corrections without overstepping.

Definitions.

Constraint – According to Merriam-Webster's Online Dictionary (www.m-w.com), "constraint" is defined as the state of being checked, restricted, or compelled to avoid or perform some action. For this chapter, "constraint" is defined as the conditions necessary to maintain the structure of the business plan. Effectively, the real or psychological areas that a business should avoid entering.

Limitation – According to Merriam-Webster's Online Dictionary, "limitation" is the quality or state of being bound, restrained, or confined. For the purposes of this chapter, "limitation" is the conditions in which the author defines the shape of the "box."

Vision – The long-term objective of an organization. It is the best interpretation of what the business can be.

Rational Action Theory – The suggestion that a person may want more than is actually achievable, when, in reality, one can only achieve what is within reason. Therefore, one must conservatively expend energy, time, and/or finances to gain the maximum output.

Measures of Performance – Real and physical actions that reasonably lead to the desired effect.

Measures of Learning – Moments in time where one conducts a periodic assessment of where the business is currently and if the business is on trajectory towards achieving the long-term goals and aligned with the entrepreneur's vision.

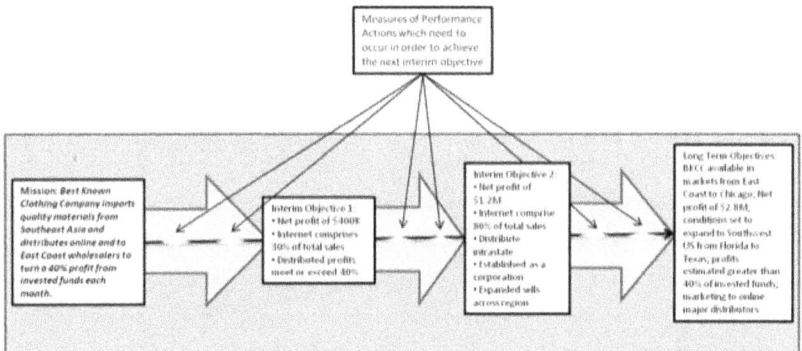

Figure 1

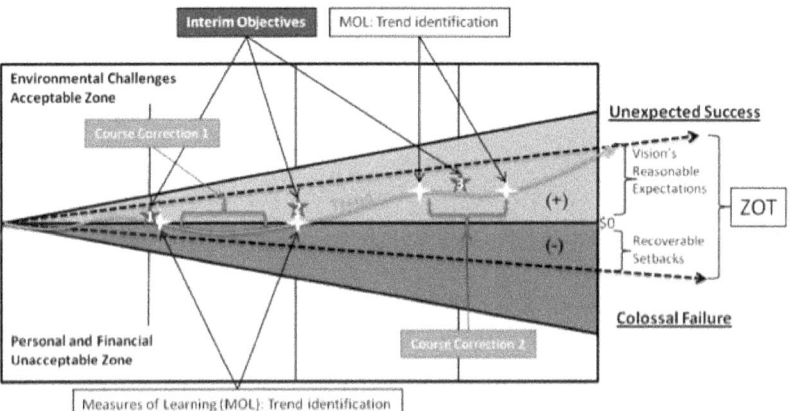

The blue line indicates the trend in which the life of the business endures.
The interim objectives 1, 2, and 3 are represented by the purple stars depicts where the owners establish as the waypoints towards accomplishing the vision.
The ZOT represents the realistic vision and the areas where
The course correction 1 shows where owners apply additional resources to steer the business out of the recoverable setback area.
The course correction 2 shows where owners apply additional resources to increase profits.
The MOL represent specific timeframes when owners reevaluate their performance and vision.
The unexpected success in the upper green are outside of the realistic vision of the business.
The colossal failure area in the lower red are the areas owners should avoid by setting realistic interim objectives, applying additional resources and establishing measures of identifying their business trends.

Figure 2

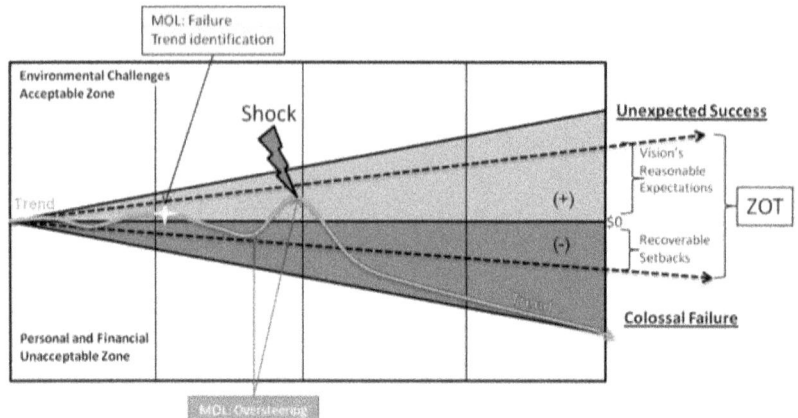

This figure displays the life of a business in which there was a failure to conduct the periodic assessment at the interim objective.
The Blue trend line shows that business begins to trend south into the limits of recoverable setback when an effort to bring the business back into the positive is observed (Oversteering)
The lightning bolt shows the shock to the business which trends the business towards colossal failure.

Figure 3

Conclusion

My son, this essay isn't supposed to take the place of me but rather to help guide our conversations and aid in your development into a productive member of the world's global culture that embraces diversity, intelligence, and determination. I set off on an agenda to help you, but through the development of this project and communication with people whom I respect, I realize the purpose of this document supersedes that of merely my son or young Black boys becoming men in urban environments; it is providing a reference for good humans with a desire to evolve with our history in fulfilling the promises made by the founding fathers of our nation...to live the American Dream!

However, despite this progress, the impact of centuries of systemic racism and discrimination still lingers. Black Americans still face significant disparities in education, employment, housing, and criminal justice. The racial wealth gap is staggering, with Black households having a fraction of the wealth of their white counterparts. We are more likely to be targeted by police, to be unfairly sentenced, and to experience violence and harassment from both individuals and institutions. Our children are more likely to attend underfunded schools and face disciplinary measures at disproportionate rates.

In addition to the lingering effects of historical injustice, such as redlining and discriminatory lending practices, continue to limit economic opportunities for people of color. This has a long-lasting impact on generational wealth and the ability to build a foundation for future success. Persevering through challenges, we have consistently shown resilience, strength, and determination to overcome adversity. The struggles and achievements of African Americans continue to shape and define the American Dream, pushing for a more inclusive and equitable society for all.

As an ethnic group, Blacks started the race of the "American Dream" 400 years behind the start line. Initially, the rules prevented us from participating because we were chattel, unequal to the human Americans. A whole nation of activists fought and persevered for civil rights to change the rules that allowed us to have separate but unequal participation. After decades, change came again and presented us with limited participation, and those rights were also infringed upon. Historically, many Americans believed the "science" that Blacks were inferior and unable to compete intellectually, athletically, militarily, politically, or socially with whites. Teaching slaves to read and write during slavery was illegal. African American communities developed their own education programs after the Civil War without State and Federal funding. African Americans were segregated and marginalized until 1949. African Americans are now ex-Presidents, Vice-Presidents, CEOs, World Champions, doctors, lawyers, vaccine developers, CEOs of top-performing companies, generals, diplomats, quarterbacks, and coaches.

Remember, as you travel through this difficult life, people will have prejudgments. They will automatically and instinctively group you into categories within the blink of an eye, as Malcolm Gladwell discusses. You will do this as well. The only thing that keeps you from becoming unaware is for you to become comfortable being aware. Money, sex, and power are the three things that corrupt completely if you become addicted. And if you become addicted, your judgment will be clouded by your addiction until you are caught.

It takes a village, so do not think you take this journey alone. If you make the trip, you didn't do it on your own, regardless of how many people didn't help, didn't support you, or didn't contribute to your cause. Trust me, they did! My mom's best friend growing up, Vernon Fay Morris, used to look at my sketches and ask me if I would build her a house. Fay inspired me to pursue architecture with that one question. When my stepfather replied to me, "Like the blind man said, 'We'll see,'" that motivated me to persevere through failures and challenges. Know your flock. Chickens aren't meant to fly, even though they have wings, whereas eagles only fly with eagles.

People always ask, "If you could change one thing in your life, what would it be?" An arrogant person would say nothing because they think they did everything right. An unaccomplished person would say A LOT because they didn't dream big enough or pursue their dreams hard enough. I've had a lot of successes in my life, but with each of those achievements, I failed so many more times trying to get it right. Every catastrophe or traumatic experience I endured has shaped me to be the person I am today. But it took reflection for me to become resilient to understand the difference between fail, good, good enough, and great!

If you expect fairness, equity, or equality, then you will be disappointed in life. Speak up and be willing to stand up when you are not being treated fairly. Stand for others when you can to demand that they be treated fairly. Sometimes when you stand up for others, you will become the target. Know when to stand! Throughout our history, our government has attempted to make improvements for underprivileged people, such as grants, scholarships, jobs, financial incentives, and education placements. And throughout our history, those who were already advantaged in life were able to remove ethnicity and those financially oppressed qualifications, to include themselves. For example, the GI Bill was initially introduced to help African American veterans returning from WWII to gain full citizenship as Americans, and became a program for servicemen and women by providing them the opportunity or resume their education after discharge.

However, that bill was changed to include all lives matter. Treating people equally is the same as believing "facts" and "truths." Facts are empirical data that can be verified by anyone, whereas truths are important. Truths are based on facts but biased by one's beliefs. If you believe someone is inferior to you, then you will treat them differently from someone who believes you are inferior to them.

These 44 points articulated in this essay are a collection of my thoughts and experiences as I evolved through life after being considered the stereotypical statistic of what almost everyone expected from Black boys in the Woodlawn neighborhood. My development exposed me to different cultural experiences that helped to shape my perspective on life. It's not that my life was exceptional or extraordinary, because many people have experienced success in their lives. What makes my life interesting is that I started by overcoming my fears, developing a purpose, and determining early on in life to be successful. My life is full of peaks and valleys, good days and bad days, but the absolute best day was today, and it will be better tomorrow.

I hope you have hope that your lives will be better!

Acknowledgements

Sonya, my first best friend. Ricky, Brenda, Linda, Gwen, and Junior for being my best cousins. Big Dog and Doris, my best friends. The men and women who served with me and shaped me.

www.ingramcontent.com/pod-product-compliance
Lightning Source LLC
Chambersburg PA
CBHW051206120626
46547CB00013B/1230